Praise for *The Holy or the Broken*

"Light is a fine companion for this journey through one song's changing fortunes."

—*The New York Times*

"Keeps the pages turning. . . . Should have Cohen devotees and music fans alike seeking out their favorite version of the song."

—*The Boston Globe*

"Ably chronicles the song's bizarre trajectory from hipster playlists to prime time."

—*Washington Post*

"Alan Light dove deep into the history of the song."

—*Rolling Stone*

"Captures the essence of a song and of the culture it was reflecting. . . . It's just so well done."

—*Christian Science Monitor*

"[A] charming ode to a pop culture phenomenon."

—*Publishers Weekly*

"Fascinating."

—*Bookreporter*

"A richly detailed study of the song's long, strange trip to prominence."

—*Milwaukee Journal-Sentinel*

"Impressive."

"Light shows how a relatively unknown song can be adopted, enhanced and canonized by the machinery of culture."

"Fascinating and complex."

"Reads like an investigative oral biography of a song. A true songography."

"Light insinuates fascinating questions about the relationship between the meaning and ownership of songs. . . . An extremely well-researched profile of the history of one of today's most recognizable songs."

THE
HOLY
OR THE
BROKEN

LEONARD COHEN, JEFF BUCKLEY, AND THE
UNLIKELY ASCENT OF "HALLELUJAH"

ALAN LIGHT

ATRIA PAPERBACK
New York   London   Toronto   Sydney   New Delhi

ATRIA PAPERBACK

An Imprint of Simon & Schuster, Inc.
1230 Avenue of the Americas
New York, NY 10020

This Atria Paperback edition June 2022

ATRIA PAPERBACK and colophon are trademarks of Simon & Schuster, Inc.

"Hallelujah" lyrics excerpted from *Stranger Music* by Leonard Cohen.
Copyright © 1993 Leonard Cohen.
Reprinted by permission of McClelland & Stewart.

For information about special discounts for bulk purchases,
please contact Simon & Schuster Special Sales at
1-866-506-1949 or business@simonandschuster.com.

The Simon & Schuster Speakers Bureau can bring authors to your live event.
For more information or to book an event, contact the
Simon & Schuster Speakers Bureau at 1-866-248-3049
or visit our website at www.simonspeakers.com.

Designed by Davina Mock-Maniscalco

10 9 8 7 6 5 4 3 2 1

The Library of Congress has cataloged the hardcover edition as follows:

Light, Alan.
The holy or the broken : Leonard Cohen, Jeff Buckley, and the unlikely ascent of
"Hallelujah" / by Alan Light.—1st Atria Books hardcover ed.
p.   cm.
1. Cohen, Leonard, 1934– Hallelujah. 2. Buckley, Jeff, 1966–1997. I. Title.
ML410.C734L55   2012
782.42164—dc23   2012036744

ISBN 978-1-4516-5784-5
ISBN 978-1-9821-4136-3 (pbk)
ISBN 978-1-4516-5786-9 (ebook)

For Suzanne and Adam,
with all my love

Hallelujah *is a Hebrew word which means "Glory to the Lord." The song explains that many kinds of hallelujahs do exist. I say all the perfect and broken hallelujahs have an equal value. It's a desire to affirm my faith in life, not in some formal religious way, but with enthusiasm, with emotion.*

—Leonard Cohen

Whoever listens carefully to "Hallelujah" will discover that it is a song about sex, about love, about life on earth. The hallelujah is not an homage to a worshipped person, idol, or god, but the hallelujah of the orgasm. It's an ode to life and love.

—Jeff Buckley

"HALLELUJAH"

Words and Music by Leonard Cohen

I've heard there was a secret chord

that David played to please the Lord

but you don't really care for music, do you?

It goes like this: the fourth, the fifth

the minor fall, the major lift;

the baffled king composing Hallelujah!

Your faith was strong but you needed proof.

You saw her bathing on the roof;

her beauty and the moonlight overthrew you.

She tied you to a kitchen chair

she broke your throne, she cut your hair,

and from your lips she drew the Hallelujah!

You say I took the Name in vain;

I don't even know the name.

But if I did, well, really, what's it to you?

There's a blaze of light in every word;

it doesn't matter which you heard,

the holy, or the broken Hallelujah!

I did my best; it wasn't much.

I couldn't feel, so I learned to touch.

I've told the truth, I didn't come to fool you.

And even though it all went wrong,

I'll stand before the Lord of Song

with nothing on my lips but Hallelujah!

(Additional verses)

Baby, I've been here before.

I know this room, I've walked this floor.

I used to live alone before I knew you.

I've seen your flag on the marble arch,

but love is not a victory march,

it's a cold and it's a broken Hallelujah!

There was a time you let me know

what's really going on below

but now you never show it to me, do you?

I remember when I moved in you,

and the holy dove was moving too,

and every breath we drew was Hallelujah!

Now maybe there's a God above

but all I ever learned from love

is how to shoot at someone who outdrew you.

And it's no complaint you hear tonight,

and it's not some pilgrim who's seen the light—

it's a cold and it's a broken Hallelujah!

FOREWORD

Tuesday night is writing night at *Saturday Night Live*. So on Tuesday, November 8, 2016, the staff started the evening working on some sketches based on the assumption that Hillary Clinton would win that day's presidential election. As the long night wore on, though, it became more and more apparent that they would need to recalibrate for that week's show.

Once the writers knew that Donald Trump had triumphed in the electoral college and would become the forty-fifth president of the United States, they were scrambling for how to handle the emotion of the country, of their viewers, of their cast. They delayed dealing with the famous *SNL* "cold open," which would set the tone for the episode. "There was no way to know what the country will be feeling like on Saturday, let alone Thursday or Friday," said writer Chris Kelly.

Dave Chappelle hosted the show that week, and he took

some of the writers aside and told them, "If it feels real, if it feels like something true you want to put out there at this moment, it doesn't matter if it's funny. Just trust what you want to put out there." They started kicking around the idea of having some of the women in the cast address the audience, speak to some of the pain and questions raised by the week and the election results, and maybe also having Kate McKinnon, in her ongoing role portraying Clinton, sing a song.

Then on Thursday, November 10, it was revealed that singer-songwriter Leonard Cohen had died in his sleep three days earlier at the age of eighty-two. The *SNL* writers had already been toying with the idea of having McKinnon perform "Hallelujah," Cohen's most celebrated composition, but they were concerned that it might feel too somber. *SNL* creator and executive producer Lorne Michaels—like Cohen, a Canadian by birth—suggested that they should follow their instincts and consider using the song.

Writers Kelly, Kent Sublette, and Sarah Schneider frantically started listening to as many covers of "Hallelujah" as they could find and researching the different lyrics and multiple configurations of verses that had been utilized since the song's initial release on Cohen's *Various Positions* album in 1984. The *SNL* staffers described stumbling across a verse that's not usually included in interpretations of the song—Jeff Buckley didn't use it in his 1994 version, which

ultimately introduced "Hallelujah" to much of the world—
and hearing it for the first time:

> *I did my best; it wasn't much.*
> *I couldn't feel, so I learned to touch.*
> *I told the truth, I didn't come to fool you*
> *And even though it all went wrong,*
> *I'll stand before the Lord of song*
> *With nothing on my lips but Hallelujah!*

"It really felt like the perfect distillation of what we
wanted to say," Schneider told Dayna Goldfine and Dan
Geller, the directors of the documentary *Hallelujah: Leonard Cohen, a Journey, a Song* (which was inspired by this
book). They sent the verse to McKinnon—who, though
she described "Hallelujah" as "the most beautiful song ever
written, one of my top three songs of all time my whole life,"
also wasn't familiar with these lines, and actually asked if
Schneider had written them for the Hillary character. Still,
they worried that at this moment of such raw emotion for
the country, the song would feel "too sad, too defeated."

At one o'clock in the morning on Saturday—now offi-
cially show day, less than twenty-four hours before *Saturday
Night Live* would go live—the three writers and McKinnon
went down to the set and let "Hillary" sit at the piano and
run through the song. And they knew immediately that,

though the show had almost never opened with a song in its forty-plus-year history, this was the right way to go.

"I'd always understood 'Hallelujah' in the context of a romantic relationship, as had most of us," said McKinnon. "And then this verse—in this moment when it was so emotional for everyone in the country, when no matter what side you were on, it was a moment of surprise and high-octane emotion—I suddenly understood it in a new light. It's about love, and how love is a slog but it's worth it."

She started to cry before she continued. "I suddenly understood it as, like, the love of this idea that is America. That all people are created equal, and that's the most beautiful idea in the world, but the execution has been long and tough and we're still just trying to get it right. But that it's worth it, and that it will always be worth it."

The nuanced layers of "Hallelujah," the sense of both sorrow and triumph, of spiritual yearning and real-life struggle, all came flowing out as McKinnon delivered the song in the middle of the night on an empty set in 30 Rock. "I think the great thing," said Sublette, "was that it acknowledged that we're not where we want to be right now, but the world's not going anywhere, and we have to move on."

"That was the tone that we wanted to set," added Kelly. "We didn't want to just come out and be like, 'Wow, this sucks. This is so sad. Everything is terrible.' We wanted it to acknowledge the sadness in the air for a lot of people, but have it be hopeful. And the song kind of takes you on that journey. It feels like it's about grief or sadness, but it also feels joyous. And at the end, singing [the word] 'hallelujah' eight times, it feels like you go on the journey of grieving this loss, and saying, 'But it's okay.' The song didn't end in a way where it felt like a bummer; there was no sad finality to it."

When 11:30 p.m. in New York City on Saturday, November 12, approached, the three writers gathered on the floor of NBC's Studio 8H to watch the cold open—something they didn't often do. "Once you're at the show for a while," said Kelly, "you're so busy and you're running around all the time, so it's very rare to go stand on the floor and watch a sketch that you write live. Usually you're running to the next thing, or you're checking cards from your sketch, or you've just seen it a thousand times so you'll watch it on the monitor. But that was one where we were like, 'Let's go down and observe this moment.'"

Dressed in her signature Hillary Clinton wig and white pantsuit, McKinnon (who said she was mostly concentrating on not messing up the piano accompaniment) flawlessly delivered a three-verse edit of "Hallelujah." At the end, she faced the camera, tears glimmering in her eyes, and she winked, and said, "I'm not giving up, and neither should you."

"That was all Kate," said Schneider. "She wanted to say that, and felt strongly that we needed a message of 'What's next?' She definitely could have sung that song and cried and been upset, but there was such a hope and a determination and a feeling of tribute and strength in the performance; it felt like moving forward."

It was a stunning moment. In three minutes, the performance captured the shock and horror so much of the nation (and, presumably, most of the *Saturday Night Live* viewership) was feeling, without wallowing in self-pity. It also allowed McKinnon and the writers to honor their relationship with a woman they had been representing in the show for many months. "It was very personal to us who had written Hillary for over a year and had been on this journey with Kate where she had really become this person," said Schneider. And it simultaneously paid tribute to the revered songwriter whose death, in light of a country in crisis, seemed all too real that week.

The episode earned the show its highest ratings in almost four years. NBC posted a clip of the "Hallelujah" performance to social media before the show had even finished, and Twitter reaction was predictably ecstatic; Lena Dunham tweeted that it was "the most beautiful thing to ever happen ever."

"In my tenure at the show," said McKinnon, "I got the most response about this one thing."

Writing in the *Hollywood Reporter*, Daniel Fienberg noted that "McKinnon wasn't really 'doing' her Hillary impression, but she was filtering Cohen's haunting song through an image of Clinton." No doubt pleasing the *SNL* writing team, he singled out the "I did my best, it wasn't much" verse.

"McKinnon's voice was cracking slightly as she sang, but I don't even know how she did that well," he wrote, adding that he watched the "Hallelujah" performance three times before proceeding with the rest of the episode. "If *SNL* had been rewriting the song to speculate on Clinton's most personal, internal reaction to her election defeat, you'd have thought that verse was too on-the-nose, but coming directly from Cohen and through McKinnon, it was almost too perfect."

In a 2017 appearance on *The Tonight Show*, Hillary Clinton herself admitted that she teared up watching McKinnon's performance. "I wish I had her talent. She's just an amazing person," said the former secretary of state. "And she sat there playing 'Hallelujah'—that was hard, that was really hard."

Chris Kelly looked back on the decision to rely on "Hallelujah," by itself, for the post-election cold open with a slight sense of wonder. "There were so many people watching and we had so many things we wanted to say, and you felt like you had to say *everything*," he said. "And if you said one thing wrong, it could be misinterpreted. There was so much pressure, and maybe we put that on ourselves, but what do you do after this insane week?

"And then when we watched it live, in retrospect it was sort of sweet how we tried to make it more than just the song. Because it shouldn't have ever been more than that."

When it was needed, "Hallelujah" was there. This was a story that I was told, again and again, when I was writing *The Holy or the Broken*. The miraculous tale of this song—initially ignored, gradually discovered, finally embraced around the world—was indicative of the undiminished power that a piece of music can have.

Working in and around the music industry day in and day out, it becomes very easy to turn cynical, jaded; to believe that things aren't like they used to be, that new technologies have cheapened and watered down our relationship to music; that it doesn't play the central, foundational role in people's lives that it once did. But hearing the stories about "Hallelujah" and its constant, recurring place in modern human experience was absolutely humbling and constantly inspiring.

Over and over, I found people who described how this song was there to serve them at their most personal, important moments—births, deaths, weddings. It has functioned the same way at significant events for the larger community, at benefits and telethons and times of national mourning or celebration. I wish I could say I was such a resourceful reporter that I dug up these stories through complicated investigations and old-school digging. But the fact is that "Hallelujah" was everywhere I looked; virtually everyone I mentioned the song to had some story about its presence in their own lives. And at these critical moments, no one talks about what show was on TV or what movie they were watching—what they remember, and what they reach for, is a song.

What is unique about "Hallelujah" is the emotional range that it's able to cover. The journey that Kate McKinnon and the *Saturday Night Live* team took with the song during those few days in 2016 is in fact a striking encapsulation of the broad-stroke progression of "Hallelujah" in the larger world. They started from a sense that the song was melancholy, almost tragic, and centered on romantic love. Looking closer, though, they found a sense of hope and perseverance, something resembling triumph in the face of life's challenges and disappointments.

Though Leonard Cohen could be reluctant to talk about what his songs "meant," this tension was what he said lay at the heart of "Hallelujah." And the slightly abstract duality of the lyrics, the simultaneous feeling of sorrow and uplift, is of course why the song resonates in times of joy and of grief. With different edits of the words, different emphases in the tone, it works at a wedding or at a funeral; its mutability allows for more options than other songs, no matter how brilliant or powerful they might be.

On August 27, 2020—the final night of the Republican National Convention—a startling mirror image of the *Saturday Night Live* performance materialized. As described by Jayson Greene in a *Pitchfork* story titled "How Leonard Cohen Haunted the Trump Era," President Donald Trump and his family "stood on a patch of blood-red carpeting at the bottom of the White House steps and gazed up at a Long Island tenor named Christopher Macchio. As he gesticulated with his swollen hands, Macchio gazed off in the distance, his mouth tugging at the corners into a Trumpian smirk. The song he was singing was Leonard Cohen's 'Hallelujah.'"

And that wasn't all. That same night, during a fireworks display over the National Mall to conclude the convention, the song played yet again, this time a recording by pop singer Tori Kelly.

The following day, Brian J. Monaco, president and global chief marketing officer of SONY/ATV Music Publishing, issued a statement simply stating: "On the eve of the finale of the convention, representatives from the Republican National Committee contacted us regarding obtaining permission for a live performance of Leonard Cohen's 'Hallelujah.' We declined their request."

The Cohen Estate released a statement, as well. "We are surprised and dismayed that the RNC would proceed knowing that the Cohen Estate had specifically declined the

RNC's use request," said Michelle L. Rice, legal representative of the Cohen Estate, "and their rather brazen attempt to politicize and exploit in such an egregious manner 'Hallelujah,' one of the most important songs in the Cohen song catalogue. We are exploring our legal options.

"Had the RNC requested another song, 'You Want It Darker,' for which Leonard won a posthumous Grammy in 2017, we might have considered approval of that song."

But there would be yet another twist during that most excruciating political season. The night before Joe Biden's inauguration, "Hallelujah" appeared once more. On January 19, 2021, at the reflecting pool by the Lincoln Memorial, gospel singer Yolanda Adams, standing alongside President-Elect Biden and Vice President–Elect Kamala Harris, concluded a somber memorial to the more than 400,000 Americans dead of COVID-19 with the song (altering the line "maybe there's a God above" to "I *know* that there's a God above").

And each time, with each usage, there were commentators weighing in, complaining that Cohen's composition was being misunderstood, misinterpreted, yanked out of context. Following the inauguration, in a story titled "It's Not a Hymn!," the *Daily Mail* wrote that the song "has been widely regarded as a spiritual hymn and has become a popular choice to sing at funeral and memorial services," but that "it's actually a sexual song—and people should stop trying to make it into something it's not." Writer Karen Ruiz quotes film critic Lindsay Ellis saying, "I'm starting to suspect that no one knows what 'Hallelujah' is actually about."

There is, of course, no easy answer to what these enigmatic lyrics are "about." The database on the leonardcohen files.com website currently lists almost six hundred versions of "Hallelujah," in dozens of languages. It's been recorded by heavy metal bands and included on Christmas records. Scarcely a week goes by that some new rendition doesn't go viral—a performance in Yiddish, in Gaelic, by a grade-school chorus or the Soweto Gospel Choir.

When I spoke to Paul Simon in 2011, he talked about writing "Bridge over Troubled Water," one of the few post-rock and roll standards that could be compared to "Hallelujah" in its impact and reach. He noted that it surprised him how "Bridge" became a song that was "permanently there" in the culture. Both songs, he said, had "found a purpose" and will "stay there, serving that purpose, until [they're] no longer needed."

Almost ten years later, "Hallelujah" continues to hold that position; if "Bridge over Troubled Water" and John Lennon's "Imagine" were among its few precedents in offering a universal feeling of gravity and empathy, nothing has risen up in the last decade to take its place. It seems inevitable that eventually something will, but maybe a playlist-driven music community has become too fragmented for a song to cut through and connect with so many disparate listeners. For now, as much as some pundits complain that the song has become too obvious or clichéd or overused, "Hallelujah" remains the go-to choice for times of strongest emotion.

With Cohen's death in 2016, the song also became cemented forever as the greatest legacy of a remarkable career. When his obituary ran on the front page of the *New York Times*, the headline identified him simply as "Writer of 'Hallelujah' Whose Lyrics Captivated Generations." His standing has only continued to grow—honors and tribute concerts and even acclaimed posthumous releases of his music and poetry proceed at a steady, ongoing pace—but it is this song with which he will always be identified first.

Nor has the influence of Jeff Buckley—whose 1994 recording of "Hallelujah" on *Grace*, the one and only album completed in his all-too-brief lifetime, was the linchpin in the song's wider introduction and embrace—waned in recent years. Since this book was initially published in 2012, three compilation albums, three live albums, and a collection of unreleased studio recordings titled *You and I* have all come out, in addition to numerous books of photos, a graphic novel biography, and a compendium of his own handwritten letters and journals. He's still regularly namechecked by pop culture's cool kids, from Zoë Kravitz to Lana Del Rey. (Despite the explosion of music biopics in the aftermath of *Bohemian Rhapsody*'s unprecedented box office success, however, the long-awaited, much-rumored, on-and-off official Buckley story seems to remain a nonstarter for now.)

In 2016, not long before Cohen's death, Bob Dylan—incredibly, the first person to really pick up on the power of "Hallelujah" and cover the song in concert, years before anyone else seemed to notice—spoke to *The New Yorker*'s David Remnick about his friend and colleague's writing. When it came to Cohen's most celebrated song, for all the attention given to the lyrics, Dylan initially singled out the music: "It's a beautifully constructed melody that steps up, evolves, and slips back, all in quick time."

It's a reminder that, as easy as it is to focus exclusively on the evocative language, mysterious imagery, and hard-fought lessons of "Hallelujah," this is a song we're talking about. It isn't a poem, it isn't just words on a page; it lives or dies on whether people want to hear it and want to sing it. After multiple decades, hundreds of interpretations, and countless appearances in all our lives, that secret chord keeps ringing out.

INTRODUCTION

The John F. Kennedy Presidential Library and Museum sits on the Columbia Point peninsula of Boston's Dorchester neighborhood. It is housed in a striking I. M. Pei building, situated in dramatic isolation on a reshaped former landfill.

This brisk February Sunday in 2012, President Kennedy's daughter, Caroline, is opening a ceremony by invoking one of her father's speeches. "Society must set the artist free to follow his vision wherever it takes him," she quotes him as saying in a 1963 address at Amherst College, honoring Robert Frost. "The highest duty of the writer, the composer, the artist, is to remain true to himself."

The occasion is the inaugural presentation of a new award for "Song Lyrics of Literary Excellence," given by PEN (Poets/Playwrights, Essayists/Editors, Novelists) New England. The award committee, chaired by journalist/novelist/television executive Bill Flanagan, includes Bono, Rosanne

Cash, Elvis Costello, Paul Muldoon (poet and poetry editor at the *New Yorker*), Smokey Robinson, Salman Rushdie, and Paul Simon. The first recipients of the award are Chuck Berry and Leonard Cohen.

The honorees are both dressed in their latter-day uniforms: Berry in a sailor's cap and windbreaker, Cohen in a dark suit with a gray shirt, topped by a fedora. In truth, the spotlight mostly stays squarely on eighty-five-year-old Berry. Paul Simon presents Berry's award—which the event program says "reflect[s] our passion for the intelligence, beauty and power of words" and celebrates these songwriters for "their creativity, originality and contribution to literature"—with a heartfelt, slightly rambling speech, reciting some of the rock and roll pioneer's most evocative lyrics, which Berry admitted at the time he couldn't hear.

Costello performs an impassioned, slowed-down version of Berry's "No Particular Place to Go," and Flanagan reads a congratulatory e-mail from Bob Dylan, who calls Berry "the Shakespeare of rock and roll" (adding, "Say hello to Mr. Leonard, Kafka of the blues"). Instead of making a speech, Berry straps on Costello's guitar and delivers a haphazard verse of "Johnny B. Goode." The whole thing winds up with Costello and surprise guest Keith Richards—perhaps Chuck Berry's greatest acolyte— swaggering through a glorious rendition of "The Promised Land," with the beaming Rolling Stone reeling off three lengthy, hard-driving guitar solos as his idol pumps his fist in the front row.

In contrast to all that firepower, the presentation to Cohen is quiet and modest. Shawn Colvin sings a delicate, slightly nervous version of "Come Healing," as Cohen leans forward in his seat and watches closely. At the end of the song, she knocks over her guitar when placing it back in its stand; Cohen graciously bends over and steadies the instrument before leaning in to give Colvin a kiss of gratitude.

Cohen's own speech is brief and characteristically humble. With Dorchester Bay and the Boston skyline gleaming through the windows behind the podium, the elegant seventy-seven-year-old talks for less than two minutes—exclusively about Chuck Berry. His bass voice scarcely above a murmur, he says that "Roll Over Beethoven" is "the only exclamation in our literature that rivals Walt Whitman declaring his 'barbaric yawp.' " He concludes with the thought that "all of us are just footnotes to the work of Chuck Berry."

Salman Rushdie's presentation to Cohen is a bit more expansive. "When we were kids, he taught us something about how it might be to be grown up," the novelist says. He quotes a few lines from Cohen's songs, and sums up his admiration by saying, "If I could write like that, I would."

Several times, Rushdie speaks of the song for which Cohen is now best known, calling it simply "the great 'Hallelujah.' " He describes the song as "something anthemic and hymnlike, but if you listen closely you hear the wit and jaundiced comedy." He gets a laugh from the audience when, with a grin, he notes Cohen's rhyme of "hallelujah" with "what's it to ya," alongside the lyric's "other rhymes equally non-sacred." Rushdie compares this "playfulness" with the work of poets W. H. Auden and James Fenton, and describes the song's "melancholy and exaltation, desire and loss."

When the hour-long ceremony is over, and the thousand or so audience members have filed out of the auditorium, perhaps Leonard Cohen allows himself a moment to smile and consider the irony. This song, which tormented him for years, only to wind up included on the lone album of his career that his record company refused to release, is now held up as "exemplify[ing] the highest standards of literary achievement." What's more, this turn of events is far from the most unlikely thing that has happened to "Hallelujah" along its almost three-decade-long journey.

"Give me a Leonard Cohen afterworld / So I can sigh eternally," Kurt Cobain once sang in tribute to the only songwriter, many believe, who belongs in a class with Bob Dylan. But "Hallelujah," which first appeared on Cohen's 1984 album *Various Positions,* has already had one of the most remarkable afterlives in pop music history. The song has become one of the most loved, most performed, and most misunderstood compositions of its time. Salman Rushdie's description of the contrasts in the lyric holds true: Joyous and despondent, a celebration and a lament, a juxtaposition of dark Old Testament imagery with an irresistibly uplifting chorus, "Hallelujah" is an open-ended meditation on love and faith—and certainly not a song that would easily be pegged as an international anthem.

"Hallelujah," however, has been performed and recorded by hundreds of artists—from U2 to Justin Timberlake, from Bon Jovi to Celine Dion, from Willie Nelson to numerous contestants on *American Idol*. It has been sung by opera stars and punk bands. Decades after its creation, it became a Top Ten hit throughout Europe. In 2008, different versions simultaneously held the Number One and Number Two positions on the UK singles chart, with Cohen's original climbing into the Top 40 at the same time.

"Hallelujah" has been named to lists of the greatest Canadian songs of all time and the greatest Jewish songs of all time (though in writing about the song for *America: The National Catholic Weekly* website, one minister mused that the singer's melancholic worldview might indicate that he "has some Irish blood"). It plays every Saturday night on the Israeli Defense Forces' radio network. It made the list of *Rolling Stone*'s 500 Greatest Songs of All Time, and, in a poll of songwriters by the British music magazine *Q*, was named one of the Top Ten Greatest Tracks of all time, alongside the likes of "Blowin' in the Wind," "Born to Run," and "Strawberry Fields Forever."

According to Bono, who has performed "Hallelujah" on his own and with U2, "it might be the most perfect song in the world."

It's impossible to determine how many people have listened to a single given song. One way to gauge popularity these days is to look at views on YouTube, which has become the world's leading on-demand music service. Totaling up the number of times "Hallelujah" has been watched on the site, it's clear that we're looking at a figure in the hundreds of millions: Performances by three different acts (Jeff Buckley, an all-star quartet of Norwegian singers, and Rufus Wainwright) have each been viewed roughly fifty million times. Cohen's own renditions of the song have another thirty million views, and four more singers top out with over ten million apiece. The YouTube onslaught is participatory, as well—instrumental versions, for karaoke, have another ten million views.

"Hallelujah" served as a balm to a grieving nation when Jeff Buckley's much-revered version was used for VH1's official post-9/11 tribute video; as a statement of national pride at the opening ceremonies of the 2010 Olympic Games in Vancouver; and as the centerpiece of the benefit telethon that followed the earthquake in Haiti.

These occasions are not always a comfortable fit for such a complex and ambiguous set of lyrics. The verses—four in Cohen's original, five in Buckley's 1994 rendition that is often considered definitive—touch on the biblical stories of King David and Samson, though they are far from pious, offering such charged language as "I remember when I moved in you, / and the holy dove was moving too" and "all I ever learned from love / is how to shoot at someone who outdrew you." Yet it also returns and lands, each time, on the reassurance and celebration of the title, which serves as a repeated, single-word chorus. The focus given to the hymnlike incantation of "hallelujah," in contrast to the romantic and spiritual challenges evoked by the verses, raises an eternal pop music dilemma: Are people really paying attention to all the words, and does it matter?

Australian composer Andrew Ford expressed his reservations about the "ubiquity" of the song. He singled out its use at the memorial service for victims of the Black Saturday bushfires in 2009, when 173 people died and more than four hundred were injured as a result of fires in the state of Victoria. "Who knows why?" he wrote of the choice. "Perhaps because its one-word chorus sits in the context of a song that includes the line 'Maybe there's a God above' it offered reassurance amidst doubt. Still, to have that response you would have to ignore most of the other words, and particularly those about spying a naked woman bathing on the roof, being tied 'to a kitchen chair,' and the verse about orgasm."

Yet to Canadian country/pop chanteuse k. d. lang, one of the most celebrated interpreters of "Hallelujah," the song has entered another realm, in which the public plays a more active role in its meaning. When she was asked to perform the song at the Vancouver Olympics, she recalls her own family's response.

"My mom is eighty-eight years old," said lang. "She lives in a seniors' apartment and all her friends were like, 'Oh, I love that song!' I said, 'Mom, do they know what the lyrics are about?' And she goes, 'I don't think they listen to the lyrics; I think they just listen to the refrain.' I think it's very indicative of spirituality in general, that something as simple as saying 'hallelujah' over and over again, really beautifully, can redeem all the verses.

"Ultimately," she concluded, "it's a piece of music and it belongs to culture. It doesn't belong to Leonard, it doesn't belong to me, it doesn't belong to anybody."

The earliest manifestation of "Hallelujah," however, could not have been more humble: When Cohen submitted the *Various Positions* album, on which "Hallelujah" appears, to Columbia Records in 1984, they refused to put it out. When the record was eventually released, the song was still generally ignored. To complicate things even further, Cohen immediately began changing and reworking the song in concert, confusing those few fans who were aware of it.

For a full ten years after its release, it gained extremely limited exposure through a few scattered cover versions. Jeff Buckley's interpretation on his 1994 album, *Grace*, ultimately served as the pivot point for the song's popularity, but even that recording took a number of years before it truly started to capture the public's imagination.

Yet by the time "Hallelujah" had become a staple for such sentimental moments as the 2011 Emmy Awards "In Memoriam" segment (performed by the Canadian Tenors), for some it was a "Hallelujah" too far. *New York* magazine's website live-blogged, " 'Hallelujah' is on the artistic ban list. Sorry, Emmys." A story on Salon.com decried the "criminal overuse of 'Hallelujah.' " Indeed, the song has been included in so many movies and television shows over the years— *The West Wing, ER, The O.C., House,* on and on—that in 2009 Cohen himself suggested a moratorium on further soundtrack placements. "I think it's a good song," he said, "but too many people sing it."

By 2012, he was a bit more circumspect about the situation. "Once or twice I've felt maybe I should lend my voice to silencing it," he said to England's *Guardian* newspaper, "but on second thought no, I'm very happy that it's being sung."

Somewhere along the way, "Hallelujah" reached the kind of rarefied status that only a handful of contemporary songs—"Imagine," "A Change Is Gonna Come"—have achieved. Its presence in the world reaches far beyond the song itself, and serves as shorthand for some greater idea or emotion.

Paul Simon wrote another one of these modern hymns. "I would not have predicted that 'Bridge over Troubled Water' would be a song that would be kind of permanently there," said Simon, sitting in the lobby of the Capitol Theatre in Port Chester, New York, on a break from rehearsal for his 2011 tour supporting the *So Beautiful or So What* album. "People used to play it at their weddings, and now they play it at their funerals, state funerals—I heard it played when Ronald Reagan died. So that song has found a purpose and it will stay there, serving that purpose, until it's no longer needed."

Over the years, Simon noticed that Cohen's composition gradually began to play a similar role, in its popularity and its uses. " 'Hallelujah' started to be the 'Bridge over Troubled Water' alternative," he said. "His song has that feel, but it's also got somebody being tied down and having their hair cut off. But it moves people in the same way that 'Bridge over Troubled Water' does, and I've heard it sung by a lot of different people, really beautifully. It's part of the mystery, that there are songs that are like that, and if you're lucky enough to be the writer of the song—well, in a certain sense, if there's such a thing as immortality, then there's a little bit of immortality attached to that."

• • •

Many latter-day "Hallelujah" fans, though, actually have no idea it's a Leonard Cohen song; they assume that it was written by Jeff Buckley. Others think that it's an ancient liturgical song, and are shocked when informed that it was written in the 1980s. Because it has reached so many more listeners through interpretation rather than through the author's own performances, now it mostly just seems like it's always been here.

Whether listeners know its origin or not, however, the mysterious imagery of "Hallelujah"—like many of Cohen's writings, a blend of the sacred and the sensual—has rendered the song something of a musical Rorschach test. Singer-songwriter Brandi Carlile, who does not hesitate to refer to "Hallelujah" as "the greatest song ever written," said that it provided her with the key for reconciling her Christian faith and her homosexuality. Carlile went through a period during which she slept with a boom box next to her bed at night; she would leave Jeff Buckley's "Hallelujah" on repeat and let it play for eight or nine hours at a time.

"To me, it really outlined how people tend to misconstrue religion versus faith," she said. "I felt that this song was, in a really pure, realistic way, describing what 'hallelujah' actually is. 'It's not a cry that you hear at night, / It's not somebody that's seen the light'—'hallelujah' is not

something that you shout out on Sunday in a happy voice;
it's something that happens in a way that's cold and broken
and lonely. And that's how I was feeling at the time."

For Alexandra Burke, winner of the 2008 *X Factor* in the
UK, "to anyone who's a Christian, that word *hallelujah*—full
stop, that's what you're going to hear." To the acclaimed,
offbeat singer-songwriter Regina Spektor, "he's using traditional Jewish stories and history, and having gone to yeshiva
and studied those stories, all the biblical things are an extra
place for my mind to go."

"I got the sexuality in the song right away," said Jon Bon
Jovi. "The chorus is like the climax, the rest is like foreplay."
For Rabbi Ruth Gan Kagan, who has included "Hallelujah"
in the Yom Kippur service at the Nava Tehila congregation
in Jerusalem, "it's a hymn of the heretic, a *piyut* [liturgical
poem] of a modern, doubtful person."

For some, it's this ability of "Hallelujah" to contain mul-
titudes, to embrace contradictions, that gives it such power.
"I can't think of another song that can be done so many
different ways," said Justin Timberlake, who performed it
at the "Hope for Haiti Now" benefit telethon. "It's a testament to the songwriting. The interesting thing that Leonard
Cohen is able to do—which equates to some of my favorite
actors—is that he never makes you choose what to feel. He
just gives you, like, a three-pronged road, and you can take
whichever path you like. That's the beauty of all of his work."

Maybe punk-cabaret artist Amanda Palmer, formerly of the Dresden Dolls, put it best. "Those verses are like the *I Ching* of songwriting," she said, "and the chorus, that word *hallelujah,* is the 'Get Out of Jail Free' card."

When Colin Frangicetto, a guitarist in the band Circa Survive, married his wife, Sam, in 2011, the bride walked down the aisle to a recording of "Hallelujah" performed as an instrumental by a string quartet. "We wanted a non-traditional wedding," he said, "but there are always family members who are more religious or traditional or whatever, and I felt like this was in a way throwing them a bone, which is ironic. Even when you take away the words, there's still a magical thing happening in the music. It's simple, but with an extreme sophistication—and I think that's the secret to most great songs, complexity hidden inside simplicity.

"It felt so fitting when committing our lives to each other," Frangicetto continued. "Leonard Cohen said the song represented absolute surrender in a situation you cannot fix or dominate, that sometimes it means saying, 'I don't fucking know what's going on, but it can still be beautiful.' "

Along with the rediscovery—more accurately, the discovery—of "Hallelujah" came a reconsideration of Leonard Cohen's standing in pop music history. After being swindled by a manager and teetering on the edge of bankruptcy, he was inducted into the Rock and Roll Hall of Fame in 2008 (at the ceremony, Lou Reed said that Cohen belonged to the "highest and most influential echelon of songwriters") and the Songwriters Hall of Fame in 2010. He has received the Prince of Asturias Award, the highest literary honor granted by Spain, and the Glenn Gould Prize in his native Canada.

A lengthy world tour, during which he turned seventy-five, saw him sell out stadiums across Europe, headline the massive Glastonbury and Coachella festivals, and play to millions of fans, of all ages. After not performing on stage for fifteen years, between May 2008 and December 2010 Cohen trooped through 246 marathon shows, to rapturous crowds and rave reviews.

In January 2012, Cohen released *Old Ideas,* his first new studio album in eight years. The record debuted in the Number One position in nine countries, and in the Top Five in eighteen more. In the U.S., where none of his previous albums had ever reached the Top 50 of the charts, *Old Ideas* debuted at Number Three. Tickets for the tour that he announced for the second half of 2012 sold rapidly across Europe and the States. Propelled in part by the ascendance of "Hallelujah," Cohen, long considered a cult artist, was finally welcomed into the pantheon of rock stars in his eighth decade.

Like Cohen's ultimate popular acceptance, the impact of the song was only realized over time. In fact, the trajectory of "Hallelujah" seems unprecedented; it is perhaps the only song that has become a worldwide standard over the course of a gradual climb spanning several decades. Only after former Velvet Underground member John Cale recorded a rearranged version of the song in 1991, which was in turn covered by the tragic young rocker Buckley a few years later, did "Hallelujah" truly begin its improbable, epic voyage.

Furthermore, in becoming Buckley's signature performance, it eventually helped the gifted but doomed artist earn a legacy commensurate with his talent: While the *Grace* album, the single studio record he released in his abbreviated life, only peaked at a disappointing Number 149 when it was released in 1994, it was certified gold in 2002 and—as a Buckley cult grew and expanded over the years—has gone on to sell several million copies around the world.

The notion of a "standard"—a song that is freed from its original performance or context and seeps into the general consciousness, where it is interpreted frequently and diversely—defined American pop music for decades. Songs from Broadway shows or Hollywood movies were the basis of most singers' repertoires, from giants like Bing Crosby or Frank Sinatra to local saloon singers. But this structure was pretty much crushed in the 1960s by the advent of the Beatles and Bob Dylan. Of the numerous upheavals these artists set in motion, perhaps the greatest revolution was the idea that singers should also be songwriters, and that their work expresses something specific and personal to them.

(It's fascinating to see the aging members of rock's Greatest Generation, the very ones who made up new rules and redefined the job of the pop singer, being drawn to the music that preceded them, and trying on the role of interpretive singers, whether it's Paul McCartney and Rod Stewart tackling pop songs from the '40s or Bruce Springsteen and Neil Young recording traditional folk material.)

R&B and country, genres that still largely maintain the traditional separation between singers and songwriters, have continued to produce occasional standards, at least within their own communities; songs such as "I Believe I Can Fly," "I Hope You Dance," or "I Will Always Love You" become part of the social fabric, turning up at piano bars, proms, first wedding dances, talent shows. But since such transitional landmarks as "Blowin' in the Wind" and "Yesterday," post-rock-and-roll pop music has seen few songs transcend their original recordings. Even "Imagine," though frequently performed in public settings, will always be so closely tethered to John Lennon's original recording that it doesn't have the same freedom and adaptability of older compositions. Furthermore, every one of these examples began spreading through the culture immediately—it was instantly clear that these were special songs that spoke to wide-ranging audiences.

Yet "Hallelujah" is different. Against all odds, it is now unquestionably a modern standard, perhaps the only song that has truly earned that designation in the past few decades. It appears in heavy metal shows and homemade videos by grade-schoolers, cartoons and action movies, *Dancing with the Stars* and religious services. It has reached a place where, for better or for worse, it is universal—even, as Paul Simon noted, immortal.

Rufus Wainwright, whose recording of the song is one of the most popular of them all, compared "Hallelujah" to compositions with an even longer history than those of the Great American Songbook, like classics by George Gershwin or Cole Porter. "With something like Stephen Foster's song 'Hard Times,' it kind of shoots out and becomes this timeless ballad that is very appropriate at all times. And I think 'Hallelujah' has that ability to be released from its shackles, and every songwriter aims for that.

"It might seem odd to most people," Wainwright continued, "but for me, being a classical music fanatic, it's kind of the way things went. Schubert's 'The Trout' or Ravel's 'Boléro'—they didn't have records back then, and people had to disseminate sheet music and sing it or play it themselves. In a strange way, 'Hallelujah' followed a very traditional path that songs used to take. It's encouraging that certain songs can still have their own lives and that they don't have to be necessarily attached to a persona, because there was a time when the songwriter wasn't necessarily the front man. I think that's the way things should be—I'm a songwriter, so I'm on the song's side."

Wainwright also pointed out that, of course, the title and chorus of the song connect it to traditions and emotions going back to some of our earliest written history. " 'Hallelujah' has been a pretty popular thing for a long time," he said, "whether it's the 'Hallelujah Chorus' or Ray Charles's 'Hallelujah, I Love Her So.' It has deep, deep roots in the human psyche. So I think it can relate a lot to different situations, whether it's about war, about peace or love or hate or whatever; it's this unifying expression of human existence, in a weird way—hallelujah—it's just life, in a sense."

"In a lot of ways, musicians covering 'Hallelujah' feel the way doing the 'To be or not to be' speech would feel for an actor," said Regina Spektor. "You become part of a tradition. The words are so expressive, the melody is so transcendent, you get to be in this incredible soliloquy and have this incredible moment. It's not like, 'Oh, Laurence Olivier did that, so no one else can.' "

How did this unconventional song attain such popularity, in such an incremental fashion, over such an extended period of time? Why did it go from being a forgotten album cut by a respected but generally unknown singer-songwriter to a track on Susan Boyle's 2010 Christmas record?

Appropriately enough, I started to think about "Hallelujah," which seems to me to be, at its heart, a challenge to personal and spiritual commitment, on Yom Kippur. Congregation Beit Simchat Torah (CBST) hosts perhaps the largest High Holiday gathering in New York City: The gay, lesbian, bisexual, and transgender synagogue is one of the last congregations in Manhattan that hold open services on Rosh Hashanah and Yom Kippur, not requiring attendees to purchase an annual membership, or even advance tickets, to attend. As a result, lots of stray Jews, music and arts professionals, journalists, and the like find their way there, and the 2010 Kol Nidre service, held in the enormous Jacob Javits Convention Center on the west side of Manhattan, drew some four thousand people.

Kol Nidre is the introductory service on the holiest day of the Jewish year, the Day of Atonement. CBST Rabbi Sharon Kleinbaum—one of *Newsweek*'s "50 Most Influential Rabbis in America" and always a remarkable speaker, who particularly rises to the challenge of the major holidays and events—gave her sermon, focusing on an interview that Woody Allen had given that week to the *New York Times* in which he said that he wished he could be a spiritual person, because it would make his life easier. After challenging the filmmaker on this premise, the rabbi ceded the stage to the CBST choir, led by Cantor Magda Fishman, which delivered a stunning version of "Hallelujah."

The unique composition of the congregation made it a little less weird to hear "She tied you to a kitchen chair / she broke your throne, she cut your hair" in this sacred context. But the notion of this song serving as the emotional peak

of the service, crackling through thousands of listeners—
who were clearly familiar with the song, many weeping as
it crescendoed—made it eminently clear that "Hallelujah"
had reached a singular altitude, and was a phenomenon worthy of some extended consideration.

When I approached Leonard Cohen about this project,
he gave me his blessing to proceed through his manager,
but declined requests to talk about "Hallelujah." And really,
who can blame him? Aside from the fact that he seldom does
interviews, even on the rare occasions when he has an album
to promote, why would he want to disturb the mythology
around this song? Having watched his composition unexpectedly attain such iconic status, largely without his own
involvement, Cohen is wise to allow the song to retain as
much mystery as possible.

In a 2008 BBC Radio 2 documentary about "Hallelujah"
titled *The Fourth, The Fifth, The Minor Fall,* Guy Garvey of
the British band Elbow recalled watching Cohen perform
the song at the Glastonbury Festival. From his spot on the
side of the stage, Garvey said that just before starting the
introduction, Cohen turned to his band and said, "Let her
go!" And that's just what's he's done with this astonishing
song—he's let it go, to find its own way, through one of the
most unexpected and triumphant sagas in the history of
popular music.

CHAPTER ONE

Allen Ginsberg once said, "Dylan blew everybody's mind, except Leonard's."

Comparisons are often drawn between Leonard Cohen and Bob Dylan. There are books devoted to comparing and contrasting the two towering singer-songwriters; in early 2012, someone even released a "Cohen and Dylan" app, documenting their recordings and set lists for comparative purposes, complete with "quiz mode." (One especially free-thinking soul—who revealed only that his last name is also Cohen—even devoted a website, WhoWroteHallelujah.com, to a detailed "musical conspiracy" theory alleging that Dylan was the primary author of Cohen's best-known song; even in the Wild West of the Internet, the site didn't stay up for long.)

The two artists have in fact crossed paths many times. They were both signed to Columbia Records by the legendary A&R executive John Hammond; both lived in New

York's Chelsea Hotel, and later wrote about it in song; both recorded in Nashville. Dylan sang backup on "Don't Go Home with Your Hard-On," from Cohen's 1977 *Death of a Ladies' Man* album. In December 1975, when Dylan's Rolling Thunder Revue tour played in Montreal, he dedicated the night's performance of "Isis" to hometown hero Cohen, who was in the audience—and then delivered the definitive rendition of the song, as documented in the 1978 film *Renaldo and Clara*.

So it isn't too surprising that when Cohen and Dylan were both on tour in the mid-1980s and found themselves in Paris at the same time, they decided to meet at a café. At this impromptu summit, Dylan expressed his admiration for one of Cohen's new songs, the largely unknown "Hallelujah." The discussion that followed has passed into myth among fans of both singers, and the details frequently change in the retellings over the years, but here's the way Cohen recounted it in an interview with Paul Zollo in 1992:

"Dylan and I were having coffee the day after his concert in Paris a few years ago . . . and he asked me how long it took to write ['Hallelujah']. And I told him a couple of years. I lied, actually. It was more than a couple of years.

"Then I praised a song of his, 'I and I,' and asked him how long it had taken and he said, 'Fifteen minutes.' "

Although clearly a story told for laughs, playing on the contrast between Cohen's meticulous, obsessive lyric writing and Dylan's notorious impatience, there seems to be a good bit of truth to it: Over the years, Cohen has repeatedly described the agony that this one composition gave him. "I filled two notebooks," he once said, "and I remember being in the Royalton Hotel [in New York], on the carpet in my underwear, banging my head on the floor and saying, 'I can't finish this song.' "

When *Old Ideas* came out in 2012, Cohen chose not to do interviews to promote the album. Instead, he appeared at a few listening events in major cities before the release date, allowing journalists to hear the album in full and then taking questions for a brief session. In London, the playback was held in the basement of a Mayfair hotel, and Jarvis Cocker, debonair front man of the band Pulp, served as the moderator. These many years later, Cohen was still talking about the torment that "Hallelujah" caused him.

"I wrote 'Hallelujah' over the space of at least four years," he said (elsewhere, he has also said that it was "at least five years"). "I wrote many, many verses. I don't know if it was eighty, maybe more or a little less.

"The trouble—it's not the world's trouble, and it's a tiny trouble, I don't want you to think that this is a significant trouble—my tiny trouble is that before I can discard a verse, I have to write it. I have to work on it, and I have to polish it and bring it to as close to finished as I can. It's only then that I can discard it."

This doesn't seem to be an uncommon situation for Cohen. In the one extensive interview he consented to prior to the release of *Old Ideas,* for the British music magazine *Mojo,* he told Sylvie Simmons, who was also in the process of writing her Cohen biography, *I'm Your Man,* of an unfinished song that he had been working on for years. "I've got the melody, and it's a guitar tune, a really good tune, and I have tried year after year to find the right words," he said. "The song bothers me so much that I've actually started a journal chronicling my failures to address this obsessive concern with this melody. I would really like to have it on the next record, but I felt that for the past two or three records, maybe four."

Cohen played another melody for Simmons on the synthesizer, saying it was something he had been struggling with for "five or ten years." He told her that the new song "The Treaty" has been around "easily for fifteen years," while he had been working on another, "Born in Chains," since 1988.

"It's not the siege of Stalingrad," he said, "but these are hard nuts to crack."

By the time he was torturing himself with "Hallelujah," Leonard Cohen already had a long, storied, and somewhat baffling career. Cohen was born in 1934 and raised in the prosperous Westmount section of Montreal, the son of a successful clothing retailer who died when Leonard was nine years old.

"I wasn't terribly interested in music," he told Simmons. "I liked the music in the synagogue. And my mother sang beautifully. . . . I first started to get interested in song when I came across the Socialist folk singers around Montreal." In 1951, he began attending McGill University; during his college years, he formed a country-western trio called the Buckskin Boys, in addition to serving as president of the debating union and of the Jewish fraternity Zeta Beta Tau.

My father was a classmate of Cohen's at McGill. Though his own premed studies didn't lead him to cross paths with Cohen in a poetry class, he makes it sound like everyone—certainly everyone among the small Jewish community, limited at the time by strict admissions quotas—knew the burgeoning campus celebrity. It was hard to miss one of their own who was straddling two worlds, receiving honors at school and performing at the local coffeehouses.

At McGill, Cohen won the Chester MacNaughton Prize for Creative Writing, for a series of four poems titled "Thoughts of a Landsman." He graduated in 1955, and his first book of poetry, *Let Us Compare Mythologies,* was published the following year.

Over the next decade, he moved to New York (where he hung around the edges of Andy Warhol's "Factory" scene), then back to Montreal. In 1960 he bought a house—with no electricity, plumbing, or telephone—on the Greek island of Hydra, living off of his inheritance while writing poetry and fiction. Cohen's 1966 novel *Beautiful Losers* was perhaps his best-known work, partly because of the book's explicit sex scenes. "James Joyce is not dead. He is living in Montreal under the name of Cohen," wrote the *Boston Globe,* while the *Toronto Star*'s Robert Fulford called *Losers* "the most revolting book ever written in Canada . . . an important failure. At the same time it is probably the most interesting Canadian book of the year."

Still, the book only sold a few thousand copies. Frustrated by his lack of success as a writer, in 1967 Cohen decided to take his shot at a profession in music. He planned to move to Nashville, but stopped in New York City along the way to meet with a potential manager named Mary Martin, a fellow Canadian who had been working with Dylan's manager, Albert Grossman. Martin introduced Cohen to a singer named Judy Collins, and he sang her a song he had written called "Suzanne." She quickly recorded it, in what would turn out to be the first of many versions of this composition.

"He told Mary that he had written some songs, and now he wanted to come down to New York and ask me if I thought that they were songs," Collins said in 2010, prior to singing "Suzanne" as part of the ceremony inducting Cohen into the Songwriters Hall of Fame. "So he sat down and he said, 'I can't sing and I can't play the guitar and I don't know if this is a song.' So he played it for me, and I said, 'Well, Leonard, it is a song, and I'm recording it tomorrow.' "

Bolstered by this vote of confidence, Cohen recorded a demo tape in Martin's bathroom, which she took to John Hammond at Columbia Records. Hammond had worked with everyone from Count Basie to Billie Holiday to, later, Bruce Springsteen and Stevie Ray Vaughan; when Dylan's first album flopped, he was known around the Columbia offices as "Hammond's Folly." In 1967, Hammond signed Cohen, who was already on the far side of thirty years old, to the label and brought him into the studio.

Cohen clashed with producer John Simon about the arrangements, and it ultimately took multiple producers, three studios, and six months to get the first album completed. He recorded twenty-five songs, ten of which made the album, nine of which still remain unreleased. *Songs of Leonard Cohen* came out in the final week of 1967. It contained several of the songs with which Cohen's reputation was made, including "Sisters of Mercy" and "So Long, Marianne," and illustrated that from the beginning, the meeting points between the sacred and the physical were central to his songwriting. (Nor was the sexuality in Cohen's songs purely literary: Over the years, he has been linked to numerous women, including such eminences as Joni Mitchell, Janis Joplin, and the actress Rebecca De Mornay.)

The album grazed the Top 100 in the U.S., and eventually became his only gold-certified non-compilation album, but it more solidly established Cohen in Europe, reaching the Top 20 in the UK. Many years later, music critic Tom Moon would include *Songs of Leonard Cohen* in the bestselling book *1,000 Recordings to Hear Before You Die.* "He transforms a common songwriter conceit—romance as a path to enlightenment, if not redemption—into an urgent, revelatory, all-consuming epic quest," Moon wrote.

Though his vocal range is limited—a deep murmur suited to dirges and lamentations—Cohen's songs were strikingly evocative and literary, with hints of cabaret, the dramatic French chansonnier style, and religious melodies. His brooding image and dark humor added to his allure, both personal and public. In addition to Collins, who would record numerous Cohen songs over the years, artists including Roberta Flack and Fairport Convention soon cut some of his material, which introduced Cohen's work to a much wider audience.

The next few years were the most prolific time in Cohen's career. In addition to touring for the first time—among these early shows was a hard-fought set in the middle of the night at the 1970 Isle of Wight Festival, during which he struggled to calm and focus a crowd on the verge of rioting (documented on a remarkable DVD released in 2009)—he released two albums that secured his standing as one of the leading songwriters of his generation. Both 1969's *Songs from a Room* and 1971's *Songs of Love and Hate* were produced by Bob Johnston, who had worked with Dylan and Johnny Cash, and he stripped Cohen's sound down to a spare and riveting intimacy.

Such classic songs as "Bird on the Wire" and "Famous Blue Raincoat," melodically simple but direct, with finely etched lyrics capturing precise yet profound emotions, defined him as a true songwriter's songwriter; the themes could be bleak—somewhere in here his songs were given the tag "music to slit your wrists by," which he has never been fully able to shake. Writing in the *New Yorker* in 1993, Leon Wieseltier, the literary editor of the *New Republic* and a National Book Award finalist, memorably labeled Cohen "the Prince of Bummers." But the accessible eloquence of the language, with a detail that's resonant but never showy, was stunning, timeless, and without peer.

Not surprisingly, Cohen has always dismissed the perception of his work as being dour. "I never thought of myself as a particularly solemn person, and I don't think my friends think of me that way," he said. "I understand over the years I acquired this reputation for being a somber chap, and of course we all go through periods where, you know, it's not that funny. But I think there's always been a perspective of letting a little light in somewhere."

As for the low, near-monotone rumble of Cohen's singing, it was certainly an acquired taste—in her best-selling chronicle of female singer-songwriters, *Girls Like Us*, Sheila Weller called it a "brazenly unmusical drone of a voice"— but he found his following. In one of his final columns for *Vanity Fair*, controversial essayist Christopher Hitchens wrote about the power of the human voice, even as he was losing his own to the cancer that would soon take his life: "Leonard Cohen is unimaginable without, and indissoluble from, his voice." British columnist/novelist Howard Jacobson wrote, specifically of "Hallelujah," that only Cohen "has a voice bruised enough to express its bittersweet lacerations."

It is a poet's voice, a sound of experience and reflection. What Cohen lacks in range is more than compensated for by his inflections and nuances. He gives little ground to pop arrangements, but his lyrics can bear the weight. Listening to his own performances is certainly more demanding than listening to others sing his words, but it is generally more rewarding as well. Producer Hal Willner, who organized an acclaimed series of Cohen tribute concerts around the world between 2003 and 2005, said, "I compare hearing Leonard to the first time you drink whiskey or beer. It's a little weird at first."

Cohen himself has been known to poke fun at his own vocal limitations. In the letter-perfect "Tower of Song," from 1988's *I'm Your Man*, he sings, "I was born like this, I had no choice / I was born with the gift of a golden voice." A few years later, he accepted a Canadian music award with the quip, "Only in Canada could someone with a voice like mine win Vocalist of the Year."

So while Cohen's early albums were hardly easy listening, the second and third became Top Five hits in the UK, and *Songs of Love and Hate* charted throughout Europe. ("I think my rise in the marketplace will be considered an interesting curiosity, that's all," he said at the time.) His star seemed to keep rising when director Robert Altman scored the 1971 film *McCabe and Mrs. Miller* entirely with Cohen songs. But as the 1970s progressed, Cohen's direction became less clear.

In the aftermath of the lunacy that closed out the '60s, singer-songwriters had become purveyors of a more personal, intimate, and reassuring expression in pop music. James Taylor and Carole King were selling records by the truckload; even such challenging writers as Paul Simon and Neil Young had become arena-filling acts. Cohen's fellow Canadian and former girlfriend Joni Mitchell created one of the masterworks of the genre in 1971 with *Blue;* several of the songs made oblique reference to Cohen, and his influence on her writing was evident.

Though his work may not be as accessible as that of any of these other singer-songwriters, this might have been Cohen's best moment to strike. But his next album wouldn't come until 1974, and it took a different musical direction. He met John Lissauer when the producer was working with a Cohen protégé named Lewis Furey in Montreal; Lissauer described the album he made with Furey as "the first punk record ever recorded, like tango-punk." Furey was playing at the Nelson Hotel. Cohen attended one night, introduced himself to Lissauer, and invited him to come to New York. After an audition for John Hammond, they set to work on a new record.

The resulting eleven songs on *New Skin for the Old Ceremony* were more orchestrated than Cohen's earlier music, with strings, horns, and a banjo, and more prominent use of (mostly female) backup vocalists. Despite such remarkable songs as "Chelsea Hotel #2" and "Who by Fire," with lyrics based on a prayer from the Yom Kippur service, *New Skin* seemed to confuse some of Cohen's limited but devoted fan base. Reviews were a bit less glowing than he was used to. It was his first album that failed to reach the U.S. charts at all, and sales slipped in other countries.

He toured throughout 1974 and 1975, first in Europe and then in the U.S. and Canada, with a band led by Lissauer. "We did this big tour, which was really successful," said Lissauer. "Then Leonard said, 'Let's write a record together,' so we wrote a bunch of songs, went on the road again doing those songs plus the other stuff, and went in the studio and got half an album done. And then Leonard disappeared."

Without so much as a word to Lissauer, Cohen put out a *Best of* collection in 1975, and returned to the road with a new band. He continued trying out new material, then went back into the studio in the unlikeliest of settings. Heading to Los Angeles, he began work on a new project with brilliant, demented producer Phil Spector; Lissauer maintains that the pairing was part of a larger deal with Columbia made by Cohen's manager at the time, Marty Machat.

Things got off to a rousing start when Cohen and Spector wrote a dozen songs together over the course of three alcohol-fueled weeks. But once the recording sessions started, it all fell apart—culminating with Spector allegedly threatening his collaborator with a firearm. (He reportedly brandished guns in the studio with John Lennon and the Ramones, as well, and was sentenced to prison in 2009 following his conviction in the shooting death of actress Lana Clarkson at his home.)

"I was flipped out at the time," Cohen said later, "and he certainly was flipped out. For me, the expression was withdrawal and melancholy, and for him, megalomania and insanity and a devotion to armaments that was really intolerable. In the state that he found himself, which was post-Wagnerian, I would say Hitlerian, the atmosphere was one of guns—the music was a subsidiary enterprise. . . .

"At a certain point Phil approached me with a bottle of kosher red wine in one hand and a .45 in the other, put his arm around my shoulder and shoved the revolver into my neck and said, 'Leonard, I love you.' I said, 'I hope you do, Phil.'"

They argued about songs and arrangements, and Spector eventually barred Cohen from the studio and mixed the album by himself. He buried Cohen's voice under his signature "Wall of Sound" production, resulting in an incongruous, if sometimes fascinating, mess. When *Death of a Ladies' Man* was released in 1977, Cohen called the album "grotesque" and a "catastrophe." *Rolling Stone*'s review was titled "Leonard Cohen's Doo-Wop Nightmare"; critic Paul Nelson, long a missionary when it came to Cohen's work, struggled to defend the album, describing it as "the world's most flamboyant extrovert producing and arranging the world's most fatalistic introvert."

Cohen retrenched coming off this debacle. With 1979's *Recent Songs*, he received coproduction credit for the first time. This set of songs added more international sounds, such as an oud, a Gypsy violin, and a mariachi band. Cohen's current touring band, the jazz-fusion group Passenger, played on four of the tracks. The album included one song, "Came So Far for Beauty," that was a finished recording from the abandoned second album with John Lissauer, and two others ("The Traitor" and "The Smokey Life") that had been started during those sessions.

It was an interesting midpoint for Cohen to attempt,

poised between the overblown Spector arrangements and the starkness of his earlier work. The lyrics were more ironic and bemused than those of the past few albums, which had been so full of bitterness. But while the Gypsy-style instrumentation added some interest, the melodies on *Recent Songs* were not his strongest, and the album seemed to lack the confidence and momentum of his best work.

The album won back some of the sympathetic press, but Cohen still felt out of step with the times. "People forget that it was against the law to listen to Leonard in the days of punk," said Bono, who recalled wanting to attend a Cohen concert as a teenager but being unable to afford a ticket. "Some of the most brutal, eye-gouging music criticism was directed at him in those years."

He soldiered on with more touring, and then a few side projects—*Night Magic*, a musical cowritten with Lewis Furey, and an album of poetry recitation that was never finished. Five years passed after *Recent Songs;* time was stretching longer and longer between new Leonard Cohen releases, a pattern that would continue for the remainder of his career. And then in 1984, after he hadn't heard from Cohen in eight years or so, John Lissauer's phone rang. "Hey, man," purred the voice on the other end of the line. "Wanna work?"

CHAPTER TWO

In June 1984, Cohen and Lissauer recorded the album that would become *Various Positions* in New York's Quadrasonic Sound studios. In the album's arrangements, for the first time on Cohen's recordings, synthesizers were prominent; they would come to define his sound more and more in the years to come. A group of musicians from Tulsa provided the backbone of the arrangements. Sid McGinnis—who joined the band at *Late Night with David Letterman* that same year and has remained with the show ever since, in addition to recording with the likes of Bob Dylan, David Bowie, and Dire Straits—provided additional guitar parts.

Jennifer Warnes, who had sung backup with Cohen on previous albums and tours, was brought further into the spotlight as a featured vocalist, a counterpoint to the limited parameters of Cohen's voice. Hawaiian-born Anjani Thomas was one of the backup singers on these sessions; she would go on to become Cohen's longtime companion, and he produced an album of her singing his songs, *Blue Alert,* in 2006.

Lissauer, a Yale graduate who has gone on to a successful career scoring films, beamed when he spoke of these sessions that took place almost thirty years earlier. Seated in the larger of the two studio rooms he operates from his thirty-five-acre farm about an hour north of Manhattan, he described working on *Various Positions* as pure pleasure. "I've never had a more rewarding experience," he said. "It was so much fun; we had a great time. Leonard and I got along so well it's almost scary. There were no roadblocks, no disasters; it was great start to finish—it was high art, it was just thrilling."

The songs included several of Cohen's most lasting compositions. The selections that ultimately opened and closed the album, "Dance Me to the End of Love" and "If It Be Your Will," stand among his best-loved work.

Midway through the sessions—Lissauer can't remember the precise sequence, but it wasn't near the beginning or the end—Cohen brought in "Hallelujah" to record. Whatever torment he'd been going through with the song's lyrics over the previous months and years, he showed no sign of confusion or indecision in the studio. "I think it was as it was," said the producer. "There was no 'Should we do this verse?'— I don't think there was even a question of the *order* of verses, any 'Which should come first?' And had he had a question about it, I think he would've resolved it himself.

"He's not one to share his struggles," Lissauer continued. "If he wasn't up to recording, if he was still working on
something, then we just wouldn't go in. But he'd never go in
and act out the tormented, struggling artist."

Leanne Ungar, who engineered *Various Positions* and
has remained part of Cohen's production team ever since,
said that there was a pragmatic reason he would not have
been experimenting with lyrics during the recording. "He
wouldn't bring extra verses to the studio because of time
pressure," she said. "The meter is running there."

It seems that the breakthrough in Cohen's editing—the
vision that allowed him to bring the eighty written verses
down to the four that he ultimately recorded—was reaching a decision about how much to foreground the religious
element of the song. "It had references to the Bible in it,
although these references became more and more remote as
the song went from the beginning to the end," he once said.
"Finally I understood that it was not necessary to refer to the
Bible anymore. And I rewrote this song; this is the 'secular'
'Hallelujah.' "

"Hallelujah" as it exists on *Various Positions* is both
opaque and direct. Each verse ends with the word that
gives the song its title, which is then repeated four times,
giving the song its signature prayer-like incantation. The
word *hallelujah* has slightly different implications in the Old
and New Testaments. In the Hebrew Bible, it is a compound

word, from *hallelu,* meaning "to praise joyously," and *yah,* a shortened form of the unspoken name of God. So this "hallelujah" is an active imperative, an instruction to the listener or congregation to sing tribute to the Lord.

In the Christian tradition, "hallelujah" is a word of praise rather than a direction to offer praise—which became the more common colloquial use of the word as an expression of joy or relief, a synonym for "Praise the Lord," rather than a prompting to action. The most dramatic use of "hallelujah" in the New Testament is as the keynote of the song sung by the great multitude in heaven in Revelation, celebrating God's triumph over the Whore of Babylon.

Cohen's song begins with an image of the Bible's musically identified King David, recounting the heroic harpist's "secret chord," with its special spiritual power ("And it came to pass, when the *evil* spirit from God was upon Saul, that David took a harp, and played with his hand: so Saul was refreshed, and was well, and the evil spirit departed from him"—1 Samuel 16:23). It was his musicianship that first earned David a spot in the royal court, the first step toward his rise to power and uniting the Jewish people.

"As a student of the sound, I understood the resonances of his incantation and invocation of David," said Bono, who added that he immediately responded to the "vaingloriousness and hubris" of the lyric. "I've thought a lot about David in my life. He was a harp player, and the first God heckler—

as well as shouting praises to God, he was also shouting admonishment. 'Why hast thou forsaken me?' That's the beginning of the blues."

But this first verse almost instantly undercuts its own solemnity; after offering such an inspiring image in the opening lines, Cohen remembers whom he's speaking to, and reminds his listener that "you don't really care for music, do you?"

"One of the funny things about 'Hallelujah,' " said Bill Flanagan, "is that it's got this profound opening couplet about King David, and then immediately it has this Woody Allen–type line of, 'You don't really care for music, do you?' I remember it striking me the first time I heard the song as being really funny in a Philip Roth, exasperated kind of way—'I built this beautiful thing, but the girl only cares about the guy with a nice car.' "

Cohen then describes, quite literally, the harmonic progression of the verse: "It goes like this: the fourth, the fifth / the minor fall, the major lift." This is an explanation of the song's structure (the basic chord progression of most pop and blues songs goes from the "one" chord, the root, up three steps to the "four," then up another to the "five," and then resolves back to the "one"), followed by a reference to the conventional contrast between a major (happy) key and a minor (sad) key. He ends the first verse with "the baffled king composing Hallelujah!"—a comment on the unknowable nature of artistic creation, or of romantic love, or both.

In the song's earliest moments, he has placed us in a time of ancient legend, and peeled back the spiritual power of music and art to reveal the concrete components, reducing even literal musical royalty to the role of simple craftsman.

The second verse of "Hallelujah" shifts to the second person—"Your faith was strong but you needed proof." Apparently the narrator is now addressing the character who was described in the first verse, since the next lines invoke another incident in the David story, when the king discovers and is tempted by Bathsheba. ("And it came to pass in an eveningtide, that David arose from off his bed, and walked upon the roof of the king's house: and from the roof he saw a woman washing herself; and the woman *was* very beautiful to look upon"—2 Samuel 11:2.)

In a July 2011 service at St. Paul's Presbyterian Church in Prince Albert, Saskatchewan, the reading of this story was accompanied by a performance of "Hallelujah." The Reverend Dr. R. M. A. "Sandy" Scott delivered a sermon with his explication of the David story and its usage in the song.

"The story of David and Bathsheba is about the abuse of power in the name of lust, which leads to murder, intrigue, and brokenness," said Reverend Scott. He recounted that until this point, David had been a brave and gifted leader, but that he now "began to believe his own propaganda—he did what critics predicted, he began to take what he wanted."

Reverend Scott calls the choice of the word *baffled* to describe this David "an obvious understatement on Cohen's part. David is God's chosen one, the righteous king who would rule Israel as God's servant. The great King David becomes no more than a baffled king when he starts to live for himself.

"But even after the drama, the grasping, conniving, sinful King David is still Israel's greatest poet, warrior and hope," Scott continued. "There is so much brokenness in David's life, only God can redeem and reconcile this complicated personality. That is why the baffled and wounded David lifts up to God a painful hallelujah."

Following the David and Bathsheba reference, the sexuality of the lyrics is drawn further forward and then reinforced in an image of torture and lust taken from the story of Samson and Delilah—"She tied you to a kitchen chair / she broke your throne, she cut your hair"—before resolving with a vision of sexual release: "and from your lips she drew the Hallelujah!" Both biblical heroes are brought down to earth, and risk surrendering their authority, because of the allure of forbidden love. Even for larger-than-life figures and leaders of nations, the greatest physical pleasure can lead to disaster.

"The power of David and the strength of Samson are cut away; the two are stripped of their facile certainties, and their promising lives topple into the dust," wrote Reverend

Thomas G. Casey, S.J., a professor of philosophy at the Pontifical Gregorian University, of these first two verses. "The man who composed songs of praise with such aplomb and the man whose strength was the envy of all now find themselves in a stark and barren place."

Lisle Dalton, an associate professor of religious studies at Hartwick College, noted the many levels on which Cohen's linking of David and Samson works. "Both are heroes that are undone by misbegotten relationships with women. Both are adulterers. Both are poets—Samson breaks into verse right after smiting the Philistines. Both repent and seek divine favor after their transgressions.

"I don't know a lot about Cohen's personal life," Dalton continued, "but he seems to be blending these two figures together with, we presume, some of his own experiences. There's no 'kitchen chair' in the Bible! There's a biblical irony that highlights the tendency of even the most heroic characters to suffer a reversal of fortunes, even destruction, because they cannot overcome their sinful natures. The related tendency, and the moral message, is for the character to seek some kind of atonement."

In the third verse of "Hallelujah," Cohen's deadpan wit returns, offering a rebuttal to the religious challenge presented in the previous lines. "You say I took the Name in vain," he sings. "I don't even know the name." He then builds to the song's central premise—the value, even the necessity of the song of praise in the face of confusion, doubt, or dread. "There's a blaze of light in every word; / it doesn't matter which you heard, / the holy, or the broken Hallelujah!"

"A blaze of light in every word." That's an amazing line. *Every* word, holy or broken—this is the fulcrum of the song as Cohen first wrote it. Like our forefathers, and the Bible heroes who formed the foundation of Western ethics and principles, we will be hurt, tested, and challenged. Love will break our hearts, music will offer solace that we may or may not hear, we will be faced with joy and with pain. But Cohen is telling us, without resorting to sentimentality, not to surrender to despair or nihilism. Critics may have fixated on the gloom and doom of his lyrics, but this is his offering of hope and perseverance in the face of a cruel world. Holy or broken, there is still hallelujah.

Finally, the remarkable fourth verse drives this point home, starting with an all-too-human shrug: "I did my best; it wasn't much." Cohen reinforces his fallibility, his limits, but also his good intentions, singing, "I've told the truth, I didn't come to fool you."

And as he brings the song to a conclusion, Cohen shows that for a composition that has often come to be considered a signifier of sorrowful resistance, "Hallelujah" was in fact inspired by a more positive feeling. "It's a rather joyous song," Cohen said when *Various Positions* was released.

"I like very much the last verse—'And even though it all went wrong, / I'll stand before the Lord of Song / with nothing on my lips but Hallelujah!' " (While the published lyrics read "nothing on my lips," Cohen has actually almost always sung "nothing on my tongue" in this line.) Though subsequent interpreters didn't always retain this verse, its significance to Cohen has never waned: Decades later, when he was inducted into the Songwriters Hall of Fame, he recited this full last verse as the bulk of his acceptance speech.

"I wanted to push the Hallelujah deep into the secular world, into the ordinary world," he once said. "The Hallelujah, the David's Hallelujah, was still a religious song. So I wanted to indicate that Hallelujah can come out of things that have nothing to do with religion."

"He's rescued the word *hallelujah* from being just a religious word," said the Right Reverend Nick Baines, Bishop of Croydon, in the BBC radio documentary. "We're broken human beings, all of us, so stop pretending, and we can all use the word *hallelujah* because what it comes from is being open and transparent before God and the world and saying, 'This is how it is, mate.' "

In the *New Yorker*, Leon Wieseltier would refer to the song as "a wryer sort of contemporary psalm with an unforgettable chorus." As Salman Rushdie would many years later, he also noted that "only Cohen would rhyme 'Hallelujah' with 'what's it to ya?' " In fact, every verse is built around the central not-quite-rhyme of "you" and "Hallelujah," as if the pronunciation of "you" that's necessary is a recurrent punch line built into the rhythm of the song. ("They are really false rhymes," Cohen has said, "but they are close enough that the ear is not violated.")

"I always picked up on at least two levels that Leonard's lyrics worked on," said Lissauer. "The obvious, the sexual undertones of so many of his things, and the alienation and loneliness that's often there. Plus, he was able to find unusual ways to talk about subjects that are not unusual. 'Hallelujah' had this unstoppable focus to it, and I knew right away that it was a cornerstone in his career."

Though almost everyone immediately concentrates on Cohen's lyrics, of course we wouldn't still be talking about "Hallelujah" without its simple yet unforgettable melody. It sways, gentle but propulsive, a barely perceptible waltz rhythm adding complexity to a singsongy lilt. "I might have contributed a little bit in that department," said Lissauer with a grin. "You can hear that it's not like a lot of things Leonard's ever done. He had a little help with the chords and the direction of the melody—we had worked together before and gotten comfortable doing that. But it's his song, I've always made that clear. And when we started to get the voicings and the chords and the melody, then it became blessed."

For some of the inheritors of "Hallelujah," it is explicitly the melody that speaks most strongly. Jake Shimabukuro is a young, Hawaiian-born ukulele virtuoso. He has built a huge online following through such mind-blowing, fleet-fingered performances as solo uke arrangements of "Bohemian Rhapsody" and "While My Guitar Gently Weeps"; *Guitar Player* magazine called him "the Jimi Hendrix of the ukulele." But one of the highlights of his live show, and one of his more popular YouTube clips, is a simple, direct instrumental rendition of "Hallelujah."

"To me, it's not about the lyrics at all," said Shimabukuro. "I really think that it has a lot to do with the chord progression in the song. There are these very simple lines that are constantly happening . . ." and though we were seated in the restaurant of a midtown Manhattan hotel, he had to stop to get his ukulele out of its case and demonstrate.

As he ran through the song's chords, he said, "What I like about it is it picks me up. It's very uplifting, and I think it's the way that the melody moves, the way that the chords move. This is the line that made me want to cover this song on ukulele"—he played the melody for the second half of the verse, like the lines "It goes like this: the fourth, the fifth / the minor fall, the major lift; / the baffled king composing Hallelujah!"—"that ascending line just does something to me internally that makes me feel good. You're just playing the scale going up, that's all it is, but there's something about that combination of notes . . ."

"The way the melody is structured is quite genius,"

said David Miller of the popular classical crossover group Il Divo. "It builds, it lifts, then there's always the one word coming back down. It's almost like sex—it builds, it builds, there's that moment, and then the afterglow. To go on that journey, the whole thing taken as an experience, is wonderful."

As for the sound of Cohen's "Hallelujah" recording, producer Lissauer had a clear vision of his own. He had written the arrangement and the orchestration, and those didn't change after they got into the studio. "It was effortless to record; it almost recorded itself," he said. "The great records usually do. The ones that you have to go and beat to death and get clever and do this and that, somehow they just don't have that flow."

Though the song potentially lent itself to a grand, anthemic treatment, and a note on the actual score indicates that the musicians were to perform the song in a gospel style, the producer wanted to hold it back. The drummer, Richard Crooks, played with brushes, not sticks; "we had to get strength without bashing," Lissauer said. The producer felt that a regular bass wasn't a big enough sound to match Cohen's vocals, low even by his usual standards, so he crafted a synthesizer bass part.

"We didn't want it to be huge," said Lissauer. "I didn't want to have a big gospel choir and strings and all that kind of stuff, so even when it got large it always had restraint to it. We decided to do this modified choir that was not gospel, not children; it was just sort of a people choir. We brought everyone in—the band came and sang, my ex-wife came and sang, *I* sang on it. In a way we were trying to get it to be a community choir sound, very humble.

"We didn't go for overpowering, hit-record-making strings and key changes, or any of the things that would've tweaked it. It got its strength from its sincerity and its focus. We just wanted it to be sort of everyman. And I still stand by that being what it was about—it wasn't about slickness or a gospel-y hallelujah; it was about the real hallelujah."

While this may have seemed like a simple undertaking to the album's producer, to Leanne Ungar, the recording engineer, this approach presented its own complications. "I think John knew just how special it was, because he took such care and extra time with every aspect of the arrangement and mix," she said. "For me, that song was a real struggle. I remember Leonard kept asking me to put more and more reverb on his voice. I love hearing the texture of his unadorned voice and I didn't want to do it. So I've never liked listening back to that recording, because I don't like the solution I arrived at.

"I remember wanting John to replace the synthesized guitar with a real one," she went on. "I also remember wishing we could record a large choir instead of layers of small groups. We wanted the song to keep growing bigger and bigger each chorus, but there are limitations of dynamic range on a recording, so the mix was very challenging."

Between the choir, the '80s-era synthesizer, and Cohen's studied performance, the studio "Hallelujah" is certainly dramatic, though, as with many of his recordings, it flirts with cheesiness. The production hits the goals it was aiming for, but there's a scope, a theatricality to the arrangement that puts it at a bit of a distance—as is often the case, Cohen's work feels a bit sui generis, something that a listener either gets or doesn't, and going back to this original recording, it's difficult to hear what would make the song connect to a universal audience.

For all of its elements, the most striking aspect of the original "Hallelujah" recording, beyond the lyrics, is Leonard Cohen's own vocal performance. Such lines as "I don't even know the name" or "I did my best; it wasn't much" are delivered with a wry, weary humor, creating a real tension between the verses and the soaring, one-word chorus. Those who know the song only through the covers that followed, many of which don't include this section, would be surprised by the additional complexities in the original. The singing creates the sense of struggle, conflict, and resignation that then pays off in the song's climactic, closing lines.

"This world is full of conflicts and full of things that cannot be reconciled," Cohen has said, "but there are moments when we can transcend the dualistic system and reconcile and embrace the whole mess, and that's what I mean by 'Hallelujah.' That regardless of what the impossibility of the situation is, there is a moment when you open your mouth and you throw open your arms and you embrace the thing and you just say, 'Hallelujah! Blessed is the name.' . . .

"The only moment that you can live here comfortably in these absolutely irreconcilable conflicts is in this moment when you embrace it all and you say, 'Look, I don't understand a fucking thing at all—Hallelujah!' That's the only moment that we live here fully as human beings."

They finished recording the song, and the rest of the *Various Positions* album. "I said, 'Man, we're on top of this, this is really going to do it,'" John Lissauer recalled. "'This is gonna be the breakthrough, this record is really going to be important.' 'Hallelujah' just jumped out at you, plus there was a lot of other great stuff on the album.

"And it went to Walter Yetnikoff, who was the president of CBS Records, and he said, 'What is this? This isn't pop music. We're not releasing it. This is a disaster.'"

Famous and infamous, music industry legend Yetnikoff had risen from the label's legal department to run the company, which he did from 1975 to 1990. His career (which is documented in Fredric Dannen's definitive study of the record business, *Hit Men,* and in his own freewheeling autobiography, *Howling at the Moon*) was marked by such earth-shattering triumphs as Michael Jackson's *Thriller* and Bruce Springsteen's *Born in the U.S.A.*, alongside a litany of accusations and allegations about his shady cohorts and abrasive style.

As Cohen recounted the story, when Yetnikoff told him that he was rejecting *Various Positions,* he said, "Leonard, we know you're great, but we don't know if you're any good."

Lissauer suggests that perhaps the executives at Columbia (a division of CBS; soon to become part of the Sony Corporation) were expecting something more pop-oriented, based on the early reports from the sessions. "The '80s was an awful period for real, artistic singer-songwriters," he said. "The '70s had everything from Paul Simon's solo stuff, James Taylor, Joni, even Randy Newman. But the '80s was all bands and MTV, and Yetnikoff might actually have been looking for a way to weed out the Leonards of the world."

Ungar believes that the rejection of the album was less strategic than that. "I think it was the usual reason—they didn't hear a single."

Many years later, in a 2009 interview with the Canadian Broadcasting Company about the ongoing success of "Hallelujah," Cohen was sanguine about Columbia's decision. "There are certain ironic and amusing sidebars," he said, "because the record that it came from . . . Sony wouldn't put it out, they didn't think it was good enough. It had songs like

'Dance Me to the End of Love,' 'Hallelujah,' 'If It Be Your Will'—but it wasn't considered good enough for the American market. So there's a certain mild sense of revenge that arose in my heart."

But without the benefit of hindsight, consider Walter Yetnikoff's position. In September 1984, Leonard Cohen would turn fifty. Each of his last three albums—covering a time span that reached back a full decade—had sold less than its predecessor, even in the scattered countries around the world where he did have a following. He had never placed an album in the U.S. Top Ten.

Meanwhile, as Cohen was in the studio recording *Various Positions,* the summer of 1984 was perhaps the biggest season in the history of the record business. Over the course of a few months, Prince's *Purple Rain,* Springsteen's *Born in the U.S.A.,* and Madonna's *Like a Virgin* were all released, and each went on to sell over ten million copies. Michael Jackson's game-changing *Thriller* was still riding high on the charts, more than a year after it first came out. Since its launch in 1981, MTV had become the dominant force in pop music marketing, with a reach and an impact unlike anything the industry had seen before, and now the world's biggest superstars had figured out how to take advantage of the exposure and opportunities that it offered.

There could be no arguing that record sales had become very big business, and were getting bigger by the day. Stakes were high. And against that backdrop, it's not hard to imagine that a record company might have had a difficult time knowing what to do with a middle-aged artist, of an elite but very limited stature, at this precise moment in music history. It's perhaps even more difficult to see a label executive being able to hear clearly enough to believe that the simple song with the Bible stories and the one-word chorus might go on to some success of its own. And, to be honest, while the synthesizer sounds were considered state-of-the-art in 1984, they weren't edgy enough to win over younger listeners, and they soon sounded somewhat dated.

Various Positions was released overseas, and two months after CBS passed on it, the independent label PVC Records put it out in the U.S., at the end of 1984. (Columbia would later buy back the rights to the album when it rereleased Cohen's catalogue on compact disc.) But still, once the album reached the public, hardly anyone seemed to notice "Hallelujah," the first song on the LP's second side. Don Shewey's album review in *Rolling Stone* didn't mention the song, though it noted the album's "surprising country & western flavor" and singled out "John Lissauer's lucid and beautiful production."

Lissauer had never even seen that review until I sent it to him after our interview. In fact, he had no idea that *Various Positions* had actually been released in the U.S. until four or five years after it happened. When Cohen's manager at the time, Marty Machat, broke the news to the producer that the record had been turned down, he said that it wasn't worth bothering to execute their contract—and so, to this day, Lissauer has never seen a single cent in royalties for his work on "Hallelujah," about which he seems curiously at peace. "I still survive, everything is fine," he said, "but it would be nice to actually get royalties for an album with the most-recorded song in fifty years on it."

The experience essentially ended Lissauer's producing career. Baffled by the label's response to a project that he felt so positive about, he switched gears and turned to making music for films, which he feels has all turned out for the best. But he does express regret that the outcome of the *Various Positions* saga effectively meant the end of his relationship with Cohen.

"Once they went out on tour and then we got word that the record was a non-record, I didn't see him for fifteen years," he said. "I think we were both so embarrassed. I felt horrible. I felt like I'd ruined his career."

CHAPTER THREE

In June 1988, Bob Dylan began his "Never-Ending Tour," his return to a regular presence on the road after decades of inconsistent touring. He has continued this approach ever since, in one form or another, playing about a hundred shows a year, or more, every year for almost twenty-five years and counting. Besides experimenting with the endless selections from his own catalogue, he has tossed in a mix of covers on occasion, often country or gospel standards but sometimes songs by his peers, including, in two shows that summer—in July in Montreal and in August in Los Angeles—the Leonard Cohen song he had recently praised to its author.

"The only person who seemed to recognize the song was Dylan," Cohen has said. Dylan apparently expressed particular admiration for the concluding verse of "Hallelujah," with its "rather joyous" sensibility. His performances, as heard on bootleg recordings, hew closely to the *Various Positions* recording—he gets some of the lyrics out of order, he leans into the rhymes more aggressively than does Cohen, with his sly elision, and the swing is a bit leaden, but Dylan's "Hallelujah" certainly conveys a sense of celebration and praise.

The interpretation is far from definitive (some, in fact, have listed it among the versions that butcher the song), but it has a clear sense of purpose, with additional resonance coming at the moment of Dylan's reemergence as a stage performer. And there's no way to overstate the significance of any song's first real endorsement coming from Bob Dylan.

But by the time Dylan took his shot at the song, "Hallelujah" had already begun to change dramatically. Cohen began touring behind *Various Positions* in 1985, and he soon started reconsidering the song's lyrics. He experimented with adding back and swapping out some of the verses that he had excised from the original sprawling manuscript.

Lissauer wonders if the modifications might have been a result of the album's rejection and commercial disappointment. "Leonard may well have said, 'Jeez, why was this not successful? I love this song . . .' and started to condense his process," he said.

According to Ungar, the lyric revisions are actually not so uncommon for Cohen. "I think he's toying with verses for years afterward on many songs," she said. "He was singing different lyrics to 'Bird on the Wire' during the 2008–10 tour."

By the time the song was recorded in Austin, Texas, on October 31, 1988, as part of a taping for the *Austin City Limits* public television series (it was not included in the episode, further evidence of its continued obscurity, but the recording was used on 1994's *Cohen Live* album), it had been transformed almost completely. It is considerably slower and runs twice as long as the original studio version. Though this appearance came just a few months after Bob Dylan's performances of "Hallelujah," only the final verse remains the same as that arrangement; the first three verses are all new, and express something quite different from the experienced wisdom and fortitude of Cohen's earlier rendition.

This version of "Hallelujah" has a much darker and more sexual edge. The David and Samson references are gone, replaced by a more caustic depiction of love. The mystery of the "secret chord" is gone; the song now opens:

Baby, I've been here before.
I know this room, I've walked this floor.
I used to live alone before I knew ya.
Yeah, I've seen your flag on the marble arch,
but this love, love is not some kind of victory march,
No, it's a cold and it's a very broken Hallelujah!

As a very different kind of hit from the '80s put it, love is a battlefield: "I've seen your flag on the marble arch," Cohen sings, "but this love, love is not some kind of victory march." (London's Marble Arch was initially built as the ceremonial entrance to the courtyard at Buckingham Palace.) And the hallelujah itself is now "cold and very broken."

Cohen's vocals aren't as low and sermonizing as they were in the studio; there's more melody to this rendition, a range that moves outside of the singsongy tune. With two backup singers replacing the choir, this "Hallelujah" feels smaller in scale and more intimate, and the arrangement is less theatrical and more human and personal.

The second and third verses get more carnal, and more bitter. The person he's addressing no longer shows him "what's really going on below," not like she used to. "I remember when I moved in you, / and the holy dove was moving too, / and every breath we drew was Hallelujah!"—sex and salvation are one, but it's just a memory now.

Most cynical, in the third verse, he allows that "maybe there's a God above," but confesses that "all I ever learned from love / is how to shoot at someone who outdrew you." These aren't the words of a true believer, not "the laughter of someone who's claimed to have seen the light," but of someone who's been burned and accepted that love is a competition like everything else. The duality of the "holy or the broken" hallelujah on the studio version has been cracked. Here, Cohen sings again of the "cold and lonely" hallelujah.

After a guitar solo by Bob Metzger, he reaches that

fourth and final verse, with lyrics intact from the studio version, and the joyousness that Dylan responded to now feels much more like resignation than triumph. The previous stanzas do indeed make it seem like "it all went wrong," but what else can ya do? He shakes his head and turns up his palms and says what the hell—"with nothing on my tongue but Hallelujah."

It's still a powerful piece of writing, and the sloweddown tempo was an appropriate choice for the retooled sentiment. But this "Hallelujah" is something more straightforward than the original—less ambitious, perhaps, if more precise. If the *Various Positions* lyrics were about faith as a response to life's brutality, including the ravages and mysteries of love, this edit foregrounded the pains of sex and romance, offering hope as a more defensive protection against defeat, a backstop to prevent us from giving in to despair. The more accessible, if sometimes more pedestrian arrangement, mirrored this pulling of "Hallelujah" back down to earth.

Meanwhile, as Cohen was continuing to tinker with this song, his visibility had begun to increase. In 1986, at the urging of his son, Adam, he made a hilarious cameo appearance on an episode of *Miami Vice* titled "French Twist" in the role of "Francois Zolan," a senior executive in the French Secret Service engaged in an illegal operation to blow up Greenpeace boats. He filmed a larger part, but his contribution was cut down to two brief scenes, not quite sixty seconds of Cohen murmuring in French into a telephone. The following year, his featured vocalist Jennifer Warnes recorded a gorgeous and critically celebrated album of Cohen covers titled *Famous Blue Raincoat* (once again, tellingly, "Hallelujah" was not among the songs she recorded).

Most important, the 1988 release of the *I'm Your Man* album—which brought him back into the Columbia Records fold, whether because Walter Yetnikoff saw the error of his ways or because he heard something more commercial this time around—was considered a career highlight for Cohen, raising his profile and critical standing following a full decade in which the underachieving *Various Positions* was his only new music. The synthesizers that Lissauer had introduced were now the foundation of the arrangements, creating a sleeker, sexy Euro-pop sound. *I'm Your Man* introduced such undeniable classics as "Tower of Song" and "Everybody Knows," and it became something of a blueprint for the rest of Cohen's releases to date.

He embarked on a widely acclaimed tour of the United States, and became more visible in the press. The hour-long *Austin City Limits* performance was his first major appearance on national television in the U.S., and in 1989, he also performed on NBC's remarkable, short-lived music program *Night Music* (including an astonishing duet with saxophonist Sonny Rollins on "Who by Fire"). "Everybody Knows" turned up as the theme song for young rebel Christian

Slater's pirate radio station in the film *Pump Up the Volume*. In Norway, *I'm Your Man* topped the charts for seventeen weeks, becoming his first-ever Number One album anywhere in the world.

It seemed that Leonard Cohen was finding a place in the global pop community in a way that had eluded him for almost twenty years. Still, when Columbia presented him with an award for the international success of the new album, he wryly thanked the label with the comment "I have always been touched by the modesty of their interest in my work."

Reflecting this resurgence, in 1991 the first in what would be a number of Cohen tribute albums was assembled by the French music magazine *Les Inrockuptibles*. The punk rejection of Cohen during the 1970s that Bono described had receded, and *I'm Your Fan* illustrated the impact that Cohen had quietly exerted on the alternative rock movement that had emerged throughout the 1980s and was on the verge of exploding via the grunge revolution. Such bands as R.E.M., the Pixies, and Nick Cave and the Bad Seeds recorded new versions of Cohen songs for this collection.

"Any attention I get, I'm grateful for," Cohen told the British music magazine *Q*. "I never believe anyone when they say that they want to pay tribute to me. Jennifer Warnes was saying for years that she wanted to do an album of my songs and I always took that as an expression of friendship. I never expected her to go ahead and make it. Same with [editor] Christian Fevret, who has put this thing together.

"He presented me with the idea and we ran through some group names. I didn't know all of them, but I knew Ian McCulloch, whom I've met on several occasions, and R.E.M. and the Pixies and Lloyd Cole and John Cale. It seemed like a really nice thing but I said, 'Yeah, seems like a great idea. Goodbye and good luck.' I never thought I'd hear from him again."

Listening to the album with writer Adrian Deevoy, Cohen singled out the performances by Nick Cave on "Tower of Song" ("I love that. It's weird, but it's a really intelligent approach") and the Pixies doing "I Can't Forget" ("Hear the conviction in that?"). The version of "Suzanne" by Geoffrey Oryema, a Ugandan musician signed to Peter Gabriel's Real World label, stopped him cold. "When you hear a guy singing a song like this . . . it gives you a good feeling," Cohen said.

But it would be the contribution from John Cale, who came to (a certain sort of) prominence as one of the founding members of the groundbreaking Velvet Underground, that would ultimately make the biggest impact. Cale had begun his career as an avant-garde classical musician, working with such giants as Aaron Copland, John Cage, and

La Monte Young. Following his years in the '60s with the pioneering, proto-punk Velvets, he embarked on a solo career that ranged from more delicate folk-pop to disturbingly intense, confrontational rock, culminating in an infamous gig during which he chopped off the head of a dead chicken with a meat cleaver on stage. He also produced influential albums by the likes of Patti Smith, the Stooges, and the Modern Lovers. Cale was also a longtime Leonard Cohen devotee, and his inclusion on *I'm Your Fan,* singing "Hallelujah" in a solo piano arrangement, offered a bit of an elder's blessing to the younger indie rockers on the album.

Cale has not spoken much about his "Hallelujah" over the years, but in an Australian radio interview in 2010, he explained his selection. "I remember going to see Leonard at the Beacon, in New York, and I hadn't heard ['Hallelujah'] before and it just knocked me sideways."

Cale said in this same interview that he had not only known Cohen's music, but also the man himself for a long time: "He's a droll character ... amazing." Yet he was unfamiliar with the recorded "Hallelujah," further proof of *Various Positions'* standing, or lack thereof, even among Cohen's devoted following. And so, Cale later told the *Boston Globe,* "I called and asked [Cohen] to send the lyrics. I had one of those old fax machines. I went out to dinner and my floor was covered in paper."

In different tellings, Cale has said that Cohen faxed him fifteen verses or, truer to the author's account of the song's initial length, fifteen pages full of verses. "Some of them, I couldn't sing myself," said Cale. "Some of them are about Yahweh, about religion, and reflecting Leonard's background. So I took the cheeky verses."

Whatever he was initially working with, Cale's solution was quite simple. Whether he realized it or not, he began his edit with the first two verses of the *Various Positions* version, the verses that begin "I've heard there was a secret chord," and "Your faith was strong but you needed proof," and then added the three verses that started the arrangement documented on the *Cohen Live* album. For the final verse, Cale chose something very different from Cohen's more spiritual conclusion:

> *Maybe there's a God above*
> *all I ever learned from love*
> *is how to shoot at someone who outdrew you.*
> *And it's not a cry you can hear at night,*
> *it's not somebody who's seen the light—*
> *it's a cold and it's a broken Hallelujah!*

Despite his implication that he avoided the spiritual dimension of the song, Cale sensed the elemental power of the biblical stories and languages, and returned them to the position of the song's entry point, but then undercut them with the lyrics focused on sexual longing and tragic romance.

The juxtaposition of the Samson story ("she broke your throne, she cut your hair") followed by the assertion that "love is not a victory march" is a particularly inspired bit of soldering by Cale. The shift in perspective that resulted from this edit is also intriguing—clearly the "you" who was overthrown by her beauty and the moonlight is not the same "you" who the singer "moved in." Like a Cubist painting, the lyric now surrounds the listener from multiple points of view.

Most notably, the conclusion was completely transformed. On *Cohen Live*, Cohen held on to the notion of the transcendent hallelujah "even though it all went wrong," retaining those final lines even as he jettisoned the rest of the lyrics. Cale, instead, ends his "Hallelujah" with the idea that "maybe there's a God above," but that the "cold and broken" hallelujah is "not a cry you can hear at night / it's not somebody who's seen the light." It is bleaker and more despondent, a hallelujah purged of joy.

A few subtle but significant alterations to the lyric—where Cohen sang, "it's not a complaint," Cale said, "it's not a cry"; Cohen's "lonely Hallelujah" is replaced by a "broken Hallelujah"—only reinforce this sense of desolation. Cale has kept a backdrop of spirituality, with the David and

Samson stories and the "holy dove," but has turned it into a lover's lament. If the song started its life by making a sacred concept into something tangible and physical, Cale now turned it on its head and made sex sacred.

This edit would prove to be a pivot point for the song's embrace by the next generation, even if that didn't happen through Cale's own recording. Amanda Palmer—make it "Amanda Fucking Palmer," as her fans would call her—is a powerful performer given to wearing corsets and combat boots onstage. Palmer began singing "Hallelujah" as an encore with her band the Dresden Dolls and retained it as a highlight of her set when she felt the occasion called for something special—like one of her spontaneous "ninja gigs" in Australia in 2011, when she led a DIY bicycle gang through the streets and ended her set with a sing-along to the song in a driving rainstorm.

Palmer explained why she thinks Cale's restructuring truly cracked the code of the song, and it has to do with the emotional momentum that he created. For Palmer, the line "all I ever learned from love / is how to shoot at someone who outdrew you" always leads to tears. "And then," she said, "if it's an especially heated environment, or a perfect night, or I'm really feeling it, or if the room is really on fire— smolderingly, quietly, on fire—that emotion will stick, will plateau right through the last verse."

Just as significant, Cale's musical accompaniment

replaced Cohen's choir-and-synthesizers with stark piano arpeggios, sped up from the pace of the original; it was, as writer John S. W. MacDonald put it in the Jewish webzine Tablet, "an arrangement that perfectly suited the song's tale of human frailty." The Welsh-born Cale's clipped, steady delivery gave the song an edge that stripped away any excessive sentiment. "Cale's version has menace in it," noted Bill Flanagan. "What for Leonard was resignation, in Cale is kind of like a drunk call at 2 a.m. to the ex-wife—there's a certain amount of 'Remember this? Remember this? Remember when I moved in you?'"

Cale created a more perfect union out of Cohen's unnerving marriage of the divine and the damaged, but it came at the cost of a spiritual payoff. Between the reassembled lyrics and the simple arrangement, he truly humanized the song, arguably flattening out the emotional ambiguity but allowing it to retain the mystery and majesty of its imagery. *NME* called Cale's recording "a thing of wondrous, savage beauty."

Cale's selection of "Hallelujah" and the stripped-down presentation he gave to it also seem meaningful in light of his own work at the time: Following a solo career marked by music that was often abrasive and brutal, he had taken a few years away from music after his daughter was born. This recording was part of a period of gentler and more reflective work, including a collaboration with Lou Reed, his estranged former cofounder of the Velvet Underground, and even a brief Velvets reunion in 1993.

Cale's "Hallelujah," which was the final track on the *I'm Your Fan* album, forever altered the possibilities for this strange, elusive song. Cohen himself began to base his live performances of the song on the lyrics as Cale had edited them—though crucially, he never let go of the redemptive final verse. The tribute record, a provocative but very mixed bag creatively, was hardly a commercial blockbuster, but John Cale's performance planted the seeds for the "Hallelujah" explosion that would follow.

CHAPTER FOUR

I t's a little hard to describe Hal Willner. He's a record producer who has worked with such iconoclasts as Lou Reed
(including on Reed's widely reviled 2011 collaboration with
Metallica, *Lulu*) and Marianne Faithfull. He is a longtime
staffer at *Saturday Night Live,* where he oversees all of the in-
cidental music used in the show's sketches. Mostly, though,
Willner assembles things—over the years, he has put together surprising and enlightening tribute records show-
casing the music of Nino Rota, Charles Mingus (on which
Leonard Cohen appears), Kurt Weill, and the songs from
Walt Disney films, and assembled concerts celebrating such
artists as Neil Young, Randy Newman, and Cohen. As a producer of the short-lived, long-lamented *Night Music,* he was
the one who matched Cohen with jazz titan Sonny Rollins
on national television.

The same year that *I'm Your Fan* was released, Willner

organized a concert commemorating the late, singular singer-songwriter Tim Buckley. The event, held on April 26, 1991, at St. Ann's Church in Brooklyn Heights, brought together more than twenty musicians to perform Buckley's genre-defying, free-form songs. (In 1989, St. Ann's had been the site of John Cale's reunion with Lou Reed; they performed *Songs for Drella,* their song cycle about Andy Warhol, who had brought them together in the Velvet Underground.)

Leonard Cohen had known Tim Buckley in the 1960s—both were loosely grouped with the revolutionary new generation of folksingers, but where Cohen was pushing the boundaries of poetry and lyric sophistication within a musical setting, Buckley was exploring the possibilities for the place where folk, pop, and jazz all meet. After Buckley died of a drug overdose at age twenty-eight in 1975, a small but fervent cult solidified around his music.

It was the avant-garde side of Buckley's work that was highlighted at the "Greetings from Tim Buckley" show. Performers included the punk pioneer Richard Hell, the charmingly oddball singer Syd Straw, and groupings of as many as five guitarists at a time. But the guest everyone walked away from the show talking about was a young man identified as "Jeff Scott Buckley"—the singer's then twenty-four-year-old son, who had actually met his late father only once. In his *New York Times* review of the evening, Stephen Holden wrote that the younger Buckley "delivered his first public performances of several of his father's songs in a high droning voice that echoed his father's keening timbre."

Jeff Buckley had grown up in Southern California, raised by his mother and known as Scotty Moorhead, after his stepfather, Ron Moorhead. His musical ambitions mostly revolved around his guitar playing—he had taken classes at the Musicians Institute, learning music theory and flashy heavy metal licks. He had been kicking around in various bands, playing on recording sessions, rooming at one point with Chris Dowd of the funk-punk band Fishbone. He had already tried moving to New York once, but had gone back to Los Angeles to record a demo tape, when Willner invited him to the St. Ann's show—a star-making moment about which Buckley later expressed ambivalence.

"When my father died, I was not invited to the funeral, and that kind of gnawed at me," he would tell Ray Rogers of *Interview* magazine. "I figured that if I went to this tribute, sang, and paid my respects, I could be done with it. I didn't want my appearance to be misconstrued, so I said, 'I don't want to be billed; I just want to walk on. I don't want to get anywhere for doing this. It's something really private to me.'"

Though he actually sang four of his father's songs at the tribute, including a memorable performance of "Once I Was" that closed the show, he only talked to Rogers about one of them. "I sang Tim's song 'I Never Asked to Be Your Mountain,'" he said. "It was about him having to take the gypsy life over a regular one. I'm mentioned in the song, as is his girlfriend at the time—my mom. It's a beautiful song. I both admired it and hated it, so that's what I sang.

"There are all of these expectations that come with this ' '60s offspring' bullshit, but I can't tell you how little he had to do with my music. I met him one time when I was eight; other than that, there was nothing."

Yet former Captain Beefheart guitarist Gary Lucas—who met Jeff at the St. Ann's show, and who would become his partner in a band called Gods and Monsters—noted that the elder Buckley played a much stronger role in Jeff's music than he allowed. "Tim Buckley was the major influence on Jeff," he said, "and, in fact, he knew his father's catalog backwards and forwards and could sing any of the songs just like his dad if he wanted."

After the St. Ann's show, Jeff Buckley went back to Los Angeles. But he didn't stay there for long. Working as a roadie and guitar tech for Glen Hansard, who would become a star fifteen years later with the indie film phenomenon *Once,* he found a job that took him on the road with a rock and roll band—or at least a cinematic re-creation of one.

Hansard got his first big break when he was cast in *The Commitments.* Playing the role of Outspan Foster, the guitarist in a hardscrabble band with dreams of bringing real soul music to Dublin, Hansard got to see the world. The 1991 movie may not have won him the accolades that *Once* did—"Falling Slowly" was honored with the Academy Award for Best Song, and the film led to a Broadway musical that won eight Tony Awards—but it did win the BAFTA Award for Best Film, and the soundtrack album reached Number Eight on the U.S. charts.

To promote the film, after each media screening in the States, the Commitments played a set at a party. This mini-tour started in L.A., where a young aspiring musician signed on for work as a roadie and guitar tech. Hansard befriended the kid. "We shared amps and guitars, fixed each other's gear, went to record shops," he recalled. "We were both big Dylan fans, so we connected on that level." One night in a Chicago hotel room, Hansard sang Tim Buckley's "Once I Was" and his friend said, "You know he was my dad, right?" Hansard had no idea.

When they got to New York, all that Hansard and Buckley wanted to do was knock around Greenwich Village and retrace Bob Dylan's footsteps. After returning to his midtown hotel, Hansard got a call from an old friend from Ireland named Shane Doyle, who had opened a café bar in the East Village called Sin-é (which translates from the Gaelic as "that's it"). He asked the guitarist if he could persuade the Commitments to come down and play; Hansard said he didn't know where everyone was, but he and his friend Jeff would love to stop by. Doyle penciled them in for a midnight set, and they were thrilled to have an actual gig in the Village.

"I remember singing 'Sweet Thing' by Van Morrison," said Hansard, "and Jeff came up and started singing the second verse. He got really into it and just started going— the café was packed, people were stopping and looking in through the windows from the street to see what was happening. He was instantly a star in that moment."

It was Buckley's first visit to Sin-é, a place that would assume mythic proportions in his legend. Sin-é had no more than a couple dozen scattered tables, and no real stage, just a small cleared space where a couple of musicians or poets could set up. As the name indicated, the bar, which Doyle and Karl Geary opened in 1989, was initially a haven for New York's young Irish community; U2 and Gabriel Byrne were known to visit, and Sinéad O'Connor, at the height of her fame, could sometimes be found cleaning things up behind the bar.

Hansard recalled that after the set Buckley "stayed and hung out at Sin-é, washing dishes—he always liked the idea of doing that before he went on, he felt like it grounded him before going onstage." He told Hansard that he wasn't going to continue with the Commitments tour—that this time he wanted to stay in New York.

Buckley was twenty-five years old, strikingly handsome,

and eager for experience. He threw himself fully and immediately into the city and its music community. He played and wrote with Lucas, but by early 1992, he was stepping out on his own, performing solo shows with an electric guitar at such downtown clubs as the Knitting Factory and Cornelia Street Café. Most notably, he was given a regular Monday night slot at Sin-é.

Intimate but low-key, the club was an ideal place for an emerging artist to work. As Buckley began meeting more people, discovering and exploring music from numerous, disparate sources, his Sin-é performances often seemed more like public rehearsals, with the singer trying out material by a lengthy and far-reaching list of artists—Van Morrison, Screamin' Jay Hawkins, Bad Brains, Nina Simone, Robert Johnson—and revealing an astonishing vocal range. The two-disc, expanded version of the live EP recorded at the club documents the boundless energy and rapid-fire, free-associating humor that defined his Monday night shows.

"He was trying songs all the time," said Hal Willner. "Certain Dylan tunes, Edith Piaf—he did 'They're Coming to Take Me Away, Ha-Haaa' one night. He just became an amoeba, a jellyfish; he was like a Tex Avery character all of a sudden. He swallowed everything—he was enthusiastic about everything. Mine was one of the record collections that he had access to, and it was great because he was just so hungry at that particular time to listen."

The two women who ran the arts series at St. Ann's, artistic director Susan Feldman and program director Janine Nichols, became very close to Buckley. "On the deepest level, Jeff was like a little brother to me," said Nichols, who preceded Willner in the *SNL* job and now performs as a jazz singer. "Susan and I took him under our wing, to the extent that he would allow it. At the very beginning, Jeff was the most unboundaried person I ever met—he trusted everyone. It was pure luck that we were trustworthy people, and off he went into the world."

The women also shared music with Buckley. He ransacked Nichols's record collection when he would cat-sit at her Park Slope apartment. Given John Cale's recent work at St. Ann's, at some point Feldman got out the *I'm Your Fan* album and played his "Hallelujah" for the young singer for the first time.

Nichols also lent Buckley the Fender Telecaster guitar that became his signature instrument; on the credits to his *Live at Sin-é* EP, he thanked "Janine Nichols for her guitar, and Susan Feldman for everything." (She eventually sold the 1983 Telecaster, which then passed through a couple of collectors before being acquired by Matt Bellamy from the British band Muse in 2020.) Looking back, Nichols said, "I'm kind of knocked out by this influence I had on his musical life, with absolutely no intent to do so."

Soon, Buckley began adding "Hallelujah" to his repertoire. Steve Berkowitz was an A&R executive at Columbia

Records in 1992 when he ran into Hal Willner on the street one night; Willner was on his way to see Buckley at Sin-é, and Berkowitz joined him.

"When I first saw Jeff, he was already doing the song," he said. "From that very first time I heard his version, it was basically as we know it now, fully formed in the way he would deliver it—this tempo, this pace, and, like most songs he did, it was his immediately, not a copy of anybody's version."

Yet Berkowitz added that Buckley was always striving to get even further inside the song, that he wasn't just satisfied by finding an approach that worked and sticking with it. "I thought of Jeff kind of like a jazz musician. Each performance was unique, according to his feelings that day. He'd play with a different pitch, in a different key. He would play a song with a slide one night, and then maybe never do it again. Feel, performance, emotion is what he was tinkering with. So he kept adding, shaping, reworking 'Hallelujah.'"

"I remember the first time I heard Jeff sing it," said Bill Flanagan, who at the time was the editor of *Musician* magazine. "It might have been at Sin-é, or it might have been at the Knitting Factory or someplace—but the first time I heard him sing it, I remember saying to him afterwards, 'Hey, you did the Leonard Cohen song, that was a good call.' And he said, 'I haven't heard Leonard Cohen's version. I know it by John Cale.'

"I think a lot of people didn't know the song, and just assumed Jeff had written it. And then it very quickly became the real high point in Jeff's show; it became his signature pretty early. It was the perfect song for him—because of his voice, but also because of how he looked singing it. It's a song that begins with King David, and Jeff kind of looked like Michelangelo's *David*. And when he sang it, it was as if a Renaissance painting had come to life."

Ben Schafer, now an executive editor for Da Capo Press, was working as Allen Ginsberg's assistant in the early 1990s. He went with the poet to a low-scale benefit for a food co-op in the East Village, at which one of the performers was Michael Portnoy, who would later rise to infamy as Bob Dylan's Grammy stage crasher "Soy Bomb," and whose routine that night consisted of shooting a carrot out of his ass.

Portnoy was followed by a young singer Schafer did not recognize, "with close-cropped hair and model-like good looks." He started to stomp and clap, building a beat, and eventually broke into a cover of Nina Simone's "Be My Husband." An audience member began to hoot along with him, and Buckley thought that the guy was making fun of him. "In the middle of the song," said Schafer, "he seethed in the man's direction, 'You don't have to like it, but you don't have to be a dick about it.' "

Buckley then played two more covers, "Lilac Wine," another Simone song, and "Hallelujah," which Schafer recognized from Cale's *I'm Your Fan* version. "I was absolutely floored," he said. "I felt my hair stand up, nearly shaking, breathless, couldn't believe the vocals and the guitar playing. Bear in mind that I did not even know Buckley's name at this point—I didn't know he was Tim Buckley's son, nothing. It remains perhaps the most single and pure musical experience of my life. I was actually spooked, in a way—it was that otherworldly."

Ginsberg read a poem and invited Buckley to accompany him. "He was reacting to the lines with little musical hiccups and accents," said Schafer. "He was listening intently to the words and letting them inform his improvised music. It was extraordinary, and it breaks my heart that this impromptu collaboration wasn't recorded."

After the show, Ginsberg and Schafer went to the much-beloved Kiev diner on Second Avenue, and ran into Buckley having dinner with Penny Arcade from Andy Warhol's Factory, who had been the MC at the benefit. "Allen had a funny, sometimes inappropriate way of asking very direct questions," said Schafer, "and he immediately lit into Jeff—'That guy hooting during your first song wasn't making fun of you. He was enjoying it, doing a call-and-response kind of thing. You seem very edgy. Are you on amphetamines?' "

Schafer felt that Buckley was already feeling the pressure, the sense that all eyes were on him. "Throughout the dinner," Schafer recalls, "Jeff seemed distracted, nervous, edgy, like a guy with a lot on his mind. I felt like you needed to be careful with him."

It didn't take long for word to spread through the music industry about Jeff Buckley. Soon, every Monday night, limos and town cars blocked the traffic on St. Mark's Place—at the time, still perhaps the global epicenter of cool—and tiny Sin-é was packed with label execs, journalists, and hangers-on. Everyone knew that something special was happening; critic Tom Moon wrote that Buckley's voice was "kissed with equal helpings of angelic purity and demon lust...a singer forever in search of unattainable ecstasy," and with his virtuosic, swooping tones and smoldering sexuality, Buckley and his eclectic musical sensibility became the subject of an intense bidding war among several record labels. In October 1992, Buckley signed with Columbia Records—the home of both Leonard Cohen and Bob Dylan.

As the time came to go into the studio, though, it wasn't immediately evident what kind of album Buckley should record. "We were not certain what the album was supposed to be," said producer Andy Wallace. "He didn't have a band— he was the darling of the East Village as a solo performer. A lot of people thought the album should capture that, but I didn't feel that way, and neither did Jeff. He wanted it to be a band record."

The choice of Wallace was an indication of Buckley's intention. The producer had worked almost exclusively with heavy rock bands; he'd helmed records by Slayer and White Zombie, and had mixed albums by Rage Against the Machine, the Cult, and, most notable of all, Nirvana—on their earth-shattering 1991 breakthrough, *Nevermind.*

In addition to continuing to write, so that he had enough material to actually make an album, the former metalhead Buckley also needed to settle on a band that could help make his rock dreams come true. Bassist Mick Grøndahl and drummer Matt Johnson were the eventual choices, with Gary Lucas on a couple of tracks and rhythm guitarist Michael Tighe joining later, for the record's final sessions.

In the fall of 1993, the Buckley team went into the famed Bearsville Studios, located outside of Woodstock, New York. Albert Grossman, Dylan's manager, had opened the rustic Bearsville facility in 1970, and it had been the site of work by such legends as the Band, the Rolling Stones, and R.E.M.

Though the band had been playing shows and rehearsing to get in shape for such ambitious, big-screen Buckley compositions as "Grace" (which would become the title track) and "Mojo Pin," everyone also agreed that the album should retain some connection to the solo work that first attracted such attention. To allow for maximum spontaneity, Wallace had set up an "acoustic area" separate from the band placement in the studio, which was ready to go whenever Buckley felt the urge to wander over and play by himself.

"After dinner or whenever, Jeff would just come in and run through his set," said the producer. "We tried to have some semblance of an audience, maybe six or twelve people around, so there was no temptation to stop, but just to play it all through. I wanted to record him as intimately as possible, so it felt like you were sitting two feet in front of him, which was the best place to see him in those tiny clubs."

"We didn't do 'recording sessions,'" said Steve Berkowitz, who was the executive producer overseeing the making of the album that came to be called *Grace*. "Jeff played the songs, and they got recorded. We tried hard not to have a barrier, just let him play, just be in it. To give him an atmosphere, an immediacy—like Dylan or Miles Davis, just to make music. Andy can make himself invisible, so when Jeff would go over and start to play, he wouldn't say anything, just, 'Get the mic into position and let's go.'

"The process was so developmental, no one knew what the record was going to be," said Berkowitz. "There was such a deep well of possibilities to choose from, it was such a tough task for Jeff." As the sessions continued to evolve, it was clear that Buckley needed to keep things going in the studio longer than planned. He left for a while to tour, returning for final sessions in early 1994, now with guitarist Tighe as part of the studio band. A four-song EP, recorded live at Sin-é, was released in December of 1993 as a stopgap to buy some more time.

Buckley continued to accumulate more and more material, but there was never any doubt that "Hallelujah" would be a leading contender for the final album. "There were a lot of these solo songs to sort through," said Wallace, who didn't know the song prior to his work with Buckley and had not heard the Cohen recording, "but there was never any question about this one going on the album, that it was something special. It had a magic to it, and that was there from the beginning."

Buckley returned to the song again and again in the studio; by some accounts, he recorded more than twenty takes of "Hallelujah" over the course of the sessions. Wallace recalls one version that began with an extended minor-key introduction. The final recording is actually a composite created from multiple takes, though memories differ as to how extensive the patchwork actually is: The producer thinks it was "pretty much straight-ahead," mostly one version with some fixes, while Berkowitz remembers a more elaborate process that stitched together a bunch of parts. "Even when we thought it was done, and we were doing the final mix, Jeff decided he needed to do one more overdub," he said.

The variations and refinements weren't dramatic; they represented Buckley searching for the subtleties and nuances he wanted, for a precise shading in the ultimate delivery of this song that he had come to inhabit so fully. A pause here, a breath there, a guitar fill—he was teasing out the slight changes that would express the feelings he was striving to communicate. "He didn't rearrange the words," said Berkowitz. "He simply Buckley-ized them."

"By the time he recorded it, he'd sung the song a hundred times, maybe three hundred times," said Flanagan. "He knew what he was going for; he knew what was in it. I think in a lot of ways it was the song he was struggling to write himself, and here he found that someone had written it for him."

The nearly seven-minute-long recording of "Hallelujah" that appears on *Grace* opens, unforgettably, with the sound of Buckley exhaling, immediately establishing a romantic sense of drama and intimacy. (Berkowitz noted that the breath came from Buckley's exhaustion after playing for several hours, not because he was just sitting down and starting cold.) He begins with a gentle, rolling introduction on his guitar that establishes a mood instantly, a riveting sense of focus and intensity; on the BBC, Guy Garvey noted that Buckley's instrumental introduction "moves from sorrow and uncertainty into confident, joyful chords before he has even sung a word." Sticking with Cale's five-verse structure, Buckley's guitar accompaniment slowed down Cale's piano arpeggios and built a subtly propulsive arrangement that was tender yet powerful: A full decade after its initial recording, "Hallelujah" was finally given a melodic framework to match its masterful lyrics.

Buckley's magnificent, soaring voice radically altered the feel of the song; he himself called the song "a hallelujah to the orgasm . . . an ode to life and love." Where the older Cohen and Cale sang the words with a sense of experience and perseverance, of hard lessons won, this rising star delivered the lyrics with swooning emotion, both fragile and indomitable. By balancing this slightly melodramatic reading with the simple, stripped-down sound of a solo guitar, he also avoided having the whole thing become too overwrought and risk collapsing under its own weight.

In Buckley's hands, "Hallelujah" was transformed into a youthful vision of romantic agony and sexual triumph. (Buckley actually expressed some doubts about the emotional liberties taken by his rendition, saying that he hoped Cohen wouldn't hear it.) In her book examining *Grace* as part of the 33⅓ series, in which each volume is dedicated to the consideration of a single rock album, Princeton professor Daphne Brooks called Buckley's performance "gospel music with sex, desire, and love tangled together and representing the keys to existential revelation and resurrection."

"When you hear the Jeff Buckley version," said ukulele virtuoso Jake Shimabukuro, "it's so intimate it's almost like you're invading his personal space, or you're listening to something that you weren't supposed to hear."

"It's a hymn to being alive," Buckley said in 1994. "It's a hymn to love lost. To love. Even the pain of existence, which ties you to being human, should receive an amen—or a hallelujah."

Glen Hansard—a lifelong Cohen fan, who remembers going to a Cohen concert when he was a teenager in Dublin—compares the two interpretations by way of a 1978 prose piece by Cohen titled "How to Speak Poetry." Closely paraphrasing the original text, Hansard said that Cohen's instruction was to "deliver the line and step aside. Don't lift your shoulders when you say the word *butterfly*—you are a vessel that's about delivering the words."

"So Leonard's version is typical of what he would do, but Jeff gave it wings, he lifted his chest. He gave us the version we hoped Leonard would emote, and he wasn't afraid to sing it with absolute reverence. Jeff sang it back to Leonard as a love song to what he achieved, and in doing so, Jeff made it his own. Leonard penned it, but Jeff owned it."

This interpretation came with a price, though. The dry humor of Cohen's original was gone; there was no room for this sardonic maturity in such an earnest performance. (Seattle-based music writer Michael Barthel would later lament the "sad-sack miserabilism" of Buckley's interpretation.) Buckley was exactly half Cohen's age at the time they each recorded the song, at a stage where "all I ever learned from love" added up to a very different set of lessons.

"Jeff was a very unironic guy, and Leonard's very ironic," said Flanagan. "So Jeff may or may not have thought about the fact that some of the lines had been intended ironically, or with some humor, but it didn't matter. Not when he did it. Jeff's version was—I don't want to say naïve, but it had an innocence to it.

"Leonard's reading was kind of an old man looking back, but when Jeff did it, it was turned around," he continued. "It was suddenly like a young man's first discovery of the power of sex and the power of love, and the connection between sexuality and spirituality, which is David's theme, isn't it? That's the theme of the Psalms. And so you have a song that really was transformed."

Even if Buckley's "Hallelujah" didn't deliver all of the layers that Cohen's words contained—maybe no one else's rendition could—the passion and power of his performance are undeniable, irresistible. He polished the song to a perfect shape, in a way that allowed it to connect with a much different kind of listener than the cult of sophisticates who were devoted to Cohen's less inviting sound.

"Jeff made more of a Fabergé egg out of the song," said Janine Nichols. "It's so focused and beautiful—nothing repeats, it's so full of ideas, just an incontrovertible thing of beauty. . . . It's like the song was lying there, waiting for someone to see what it could be."

• • • •

Jeff Buckley's Grace album was released by Columbia Records in August 1994, amid a flurry of hype. The final song selection included seven songs written or cowritten by Buckley; three of his wide range of covers also made the cut, illustrating his sprawling tastes and influences. The album's fourth track is Nina Simone's "Lilac Wine," a staple of his live show. A version of Benjamin Britten's "Corpus Christi Carol" comes near the record's end. Right at the album's center sits "Hallelujah," the set's longest track.

For all the high expectations, though, and the mystique it would later acquire, Grace was a flop; it didn't make the Top 100 on the U.S. charts, and only one single, "Last Goodbye," made any kind of dent on rock radio. (Buckley did, however, make the list of People magazine's 50 Most Beautiful People in 1995.) Like Leonard Cohen before him, Buckley made more of an impact overseas: Grace nicked the Top 50 of the charts in the UK and France.

Even within the limited attention that the album did receive, "Hallelujah" was far from being the focal point. Four songs were eventually released as singles from Grace (the title track, "Last Goodbye," "So Real," and "Eternal Life"); there was actually talk of releasing "Hallelujah" as yet another single, but by that time, sales had slowed to the point where Columbia decided instead to drop its promotional efforts. Feature stories and interviews with Buckley hardly mentioned the song, and its reception by the critics was mixed.

In *Rolling Stone*, Stephanie Zacharek wrote that "the young Buckley's vocals don't always stand up: He doesn't sound battered or desperate enough to carry off Leonard Cohen's 'Hallelujah.'" A year-end wrap-up in the *New York Times* offered a different perspective, though. Stephen Holden (who had covered the St. Ann's show for the newspaper) wrote that the recording "may be the single most powerful performance of a Cohen song outside of Mr. Cohen's own versions."

Some reviews for *Grace* were downright negative: The influential "dean of American rock critics," Robert Christgau, listed the album in his 1994 "Turkey Shoot" in the *Village Voice*, writing, "It's wrong to peg him as the unwelcome ghost of his overwrought dad. Young Jeff is a syncretic asshole. . . . Let us pray the force of hype blows him all the way to Uranus." But, despite its commercial failure, when the smoke cleared, *Grace* appeared on many critics' lists of the year's best albums in the U.S., the UK, and France.

More significantly, Jeff Buckley was celebrated by the rock and roll elite: Paul McCartney, Jimmy Page, Elvis Costello, and Eddie Vedder were among the stars who raved about the young singer. If he didn't quite turn into the pop star he was supposed to be, Buckley was at least a top-shelf underground celebrity. And among young listeners, especially those who were dreaming about making music themselves, "Hallelujah" was a song that was attracting some notice.

Almost a decade before her debut, *Come Away with Me,* sold ten million copies and won five Grammy Awards, Norah Jones stumbled across *Grace* as a high school student in Texas. "I went to the CD store, it was on display and it looked interesting," she said. "But I remember thinking, 'Is this a Christian album? It's called *Grace,* it has songs called "Hallelujah" and "Corpus Christi Carol" on it—that's not what I came here to buy.' But I listened to a little and it sounded kind of cool. This was when it first came out, and nobody really knew about it—hey, does that make me cool?"

She soon discovered "Hallelujah," and couldn't stop listening to it; in 2012, it was her answer in the category "First Song That I Was Obsessed With" in an interview with *Entertainment Weekly.* "It's just stunning, it's one of the most beautiful things ever recorded," she said. "I believe every word he says. I had a boom box with a CD player and a repeat button, and I'd play it over and over. I'd fall asleep to it, but when he hits that high note, every time it would wake me up, so I'd wake up every four minutes."

For Brandi Carlile, growing up in Washington State, the religious overtones of the song had a more specific resonance. "It was really *the* song from *Grace* that most jumped out," she said, during a conversation in her Manhattan hotel room, a few hours before a sold-out show at Town Hall. "Somebody played that song for me and I fell head over heels in love with it. I was having really complicated faith struggles during that time. I just had an instant connection to it based on that."

So there was the substance of the song, and for some listeners, that was the key. But there was also that indescribable essence that Buckley was trying to conjure in take after take during the sessions. The fans that reacted so strongly to this song were connecting directly with Jeff Buckley, to an intangible intimacy that certain recordings convey and a clarity that he seized on and never let go.

"A lot of musicians talk about it, but there really is something to a magic performance—it's a rare thing," said Patrick Stump of the pop-punk band Fall Out Boy, who would later incorporate part of "Hallelujah" into a song of their own titled "Hum Hallelujah," which would in turn become a favorite of their own fans. "The thing about the Jeff Buckley version of 'Hallelujah' that gave it another life was that it was just a magical performance. There really are very few of those in music history, recordings that are just dead-on—something like Otis Redding's 'These Arms of Mine.'

"Jeff Buckley had that quality, and even he couldn't have performed the song that same way again. [Cohen's] original was so produced, and Buckley's is so small, just a guy and his guitar, and he makes it so personal. . . . He was able to find so many different things in that lyric—sex, passion, darkness, beauty are all in his voice. In the end it lends itself to Jeff Buckley's legacy as much as Leonard Cohen's."

"Hallelujah" has become an unexpected staple in the live act of heavy metal band Alter Bridge, initially an offshoot of the mega-selling hard rock band Creed. (Coincidentally, on my way to meet up with Alter Bridge singer Myles Kennedy prior to a concert by his band, a cellist was playing "Hallelujah" in the Union Square subway station.)

In a downstairs lounge under the Best Buy Theater, in the heart of Times Square, Kennedy (who also sings in a band led by guitarist Slash, and filled in for Axl Rose when Guns N' Roses were inducted into the Rock and Roll Hall of Fame in 2012) recalled the first time he heard Buckley's recording of the song, saying, "It was one of those life-changing moments. I was in my house in Spokane, Washington, I think it was January of '95. I had just gotten the *Grace* record and sat down and was listening to it, and that song came on and I was completely dumbfounded. Then I got to see him perform it about five months later in Seattle.

"The thing about Jeff's interpretation is that there's a certain melancholy, a certain longing. What I got out of it was the idea of surrendering, just total surrender to this thing called love. The vibe I get in reading that lyric, or in singing it, is that it's not necessarily perfect; it's painful. But surrendering nonetheless. And it's beautiful."

Amanda Palmer, who has often performed "Hallelujah" live, takes a bit of a contrary view (as she does with most things); she said that she appreciates Buckley's interpretation more than she loves it, and finds his reading more calculated than truly organic. "I think Jeff Buckley was brilliant, but his version of the song always struck me as too technical," she said. "But I get totally why that version hooked people, because he also knows what you *can't* do with that song, which is that you can't get so overwrought that you lose the plot. You've got to deliver it just right, and he's got this angelic, fantastic, otherworldly voice.

"I think the other important part of that song is you don't fucking over-orchestrate it. You don't put swelling strings and a symphony behind it. That song works best when it's just stripped down."

Jeff Buckley's following may not have been as big as Columbia Records had hoped for, but it was certainly fervent. And as these listeners discovered Buckley, some of them were also being introduced to the older Canadian gentleman who had a songwriting credit on the album. While Buckley didn't know Cohen's work when he first started performing "Hallelujah," by the time *Grace* was released, he had become a student of the man's music.

"He developed a tremendous respect and reverence for

all things Leonard," said Steve Berkowitz. "Like Dylan, Led Zeppelin, Miles Davis, James Brown—they were all of the highest order to Jeff." Buckley was photographed holding a banana in tribute to the cover of Cohen's *I'm Your Man*, and in the booklet for the expanded reissue of *Grace*, there's a shot of him holding a copy of the *Various Positions* LP.

"The reason I did 'Hallelujah' was because of the song, and not because of Leonard," he told MTV's *120 Minutes* alternative video show. "But you can't help but admire him."

When Norah Jones first heard "Hallelujah," she didn't know that it was a cover. "Then I also realized Leonard Cohen wrote 'Everybody Knows,' which I knew from Concrete Blonde doing it on the *Pump Up the Volume* soundtrack," she said. "I also used to listen to Nina Simone's version of 'Suzanne,' so then I was like, 'Who is this guy?'"

If Leonard Cohen was the author of "Hallelujah" and John Cale was its editor, Jeff Buckley was the song's ultimate performer. A decade after its original recording, the song had found its defining voice, and the *Grace* recording would essentially become the version against which future versions would be measured.

To this new generation of cool kids, "Hallelujah" belonged to Jeff Buckley. Having honed his performance of the song in tiny Manhattan clubs, he was ready to take it out to the world with complete confidence. Often even a famous artist will offer deference or defensiveness when covering someone else's composition, but not Jeff Buckley. ("Jeff was never intimidated by a song," said Glen Hansard. "That's kind of what made him great.") He was delivering "Hallelujah" with an intensity that was almost mystic, and a very different manifestation of the ecstatic, "holy hallelujah" in Cohen's original.

Just how much he had taken on a new and specific meaning for his "Hallelujah" was evident in the razor-edged, street-romantic way Buckley introduced the song onstage in Germany in 1995. "It's not the bottle," he said. "It's not the pills. It's not the face of strangers who will offer you their lines and hot needles. It's not the time you were together in their place—so perfect, like a second home. And it's not from the Bible. It's not from angels. Not from preachers who are chaste and understanding of nothing that is human in this world. It's for people who are lovers. It's for people who have been lovers. You are at last somewhere. Until then it's hallelujah."

CHAPTER FIVE

The same year that *Grace* was released, Leonard Cohen disappeared. In 1992, his ninth album, *The Future,* came out. Released following the riots in Los Angeles in the aftermath of the Rodney King verdict—Cohen could see the fires from his house—the record expressed some of his bleakest sentiments; "I've seen the future, baby: / it is murder," he sneered on the title track, and "Give me crack and anal sex / Take the only tree that's left / and stuff it up the hole / in your culture."

The album was more scriptural, more apocalyptic, even by Cohen's standards. But it also contained some of his most profound struggling for hope—in one of his most celebrated lines, on "Anthem," he sang, "There is a crack in everything / That's how the light gets in."

"I write the songs when I get to the place where I can't be dishonest about what I'm doing," Cohen told Anthony DeCurtis in *Rolling Stone.* "The record is there for keeps. There's flesh and blood attached to it. I did what was necessary, and I sit here kind of wrecked."

Most of the interviews he did around the album's release still did not mention "Hallelujah," even within lists of his best-known compositions. (In fact, even a Cohen biography published in 1996 with the title *Various Positions* did not include a single reference to the song.) In 1993, Cohen published a collection of his lyrics and poetry titled *Stranger Music,* which he had spent several years assembling. "Hallelujah" was included with the four verses as recorded on *Various Positions,* and then the other lyrics from the Cale/Buckley version listed as "additional verses."

The Future gave Cohen his greatest commercial success in years—it went double platinum in Canada and reached the Top 40 in the UK—though it still did not chart in the U.S. Following a 1993 tour, he withdrew from the public eye and began a period during which he spent years in isolated study at a Zen monastery in the San Gabriel Mountains outside of Los Angeles.

According to its website, the Mt. Baldy Zen Center, founded in a former Boy Scout camp by Kyozan Joshu Sasaki Roshi (who is still the center's teacher today, at age 105), "enables ordained priests and lay students to train together in a formal, but rustic setting—designed to help us realize fundamental insights into our nature, and to manifest these insights in everyday life." For the remainder of the 1990s, as he turned sixty and beyond, the Canadian Jew mostly stayed 6,500 feet up Mt. Baldy, learning from the elderly Zen master, whom he had first met in 1969. This grandson of a rabbi, who has said that he has explored spiritual directions "from Scientology to delusions of [himself] as the High Priest rebuilding the Temple," was embracing a life of intensive reflection: Cohen performed ritual tasks, spoke little, and wrote only for himself. In time, he would be ordained a Rinzai Buddhist monk and given the name "Jikan," meaning "Ordinary Silence."

"There was no sense of dissatisfaction with my career," Cohen later said to writer Mikal Gilmore of his time at the monastery. "On the contrary. If anything, it was like, 'Well, so this is what it's like to succeed.' I had the respect of my peers and another generation or two, and people were writing kindly about me." He said that when he decided to study with Roshi, it was "with the feeling of, 'If this works, I'll stay.' I didn't put a limit on it, but I knew I was going to be there for a while."

In the absence of any new recordings, Columbia Records spent the rest of the 1990s exploring Cohen's back catalogue. In 1994, *Cohen Live* came out—a compilation of concert performances over the years, including the *Austin City Limits* version of "Hallelujah" from 1988. That same year, Trent Reznor, the front man of Nine Inch Nails, assembled the soundtrack for Oliver Stone's film *Natural Born Kill-*

ers, and included three Cohen songs (two on the soundtrack album)—an endorsement of Cohen's eternal cool by two new-school rebels that introduced him to yet another audience. (This came on the heels of the shout-out to Cohen by Nirvana, then perhaps the biggest band in the world, on the 1993 song "Pennyroyal Tea.")

More tribute albums were recorded in Cohen's honor, in the Czech Republic and Spain. In an interview with KCRW's Chris Douridas, Cohen said that when these records "landed in the mailbox," he was "very impressed by the performances and the treatment, and I thought, 'Who can I turn to, to let people hear this?'" He and his team decided to help assemble a tribute project of their own.

Titled *Tower of Song,* the 1995 collection reflected the fact that Cohen's star had risen considerably in a few years; it featured bigger names than the indie rockers on *I'm Your Fan,* including Elton John, Sting, and Peter Gabriel. The subject himself told Douridas that "whenever I hear anybody do one of my songs my critical judgments go into immediate suspended animation. I'm just knocked out when anybody does a cover of mine. . . . First of all, I am happy that someone has heard the song and is moved to cover it. Second of all, it gives me a completely fresh take on the song and I can then enter it into my own judgmental process." He singled out Billy Joel's version of "Light as a Breeze" as a particular favorite: "I think it's a much, much better version of the one I came up with."

On *Tower of Song*, "Hallelujah" was interpreted by one of the biggest names of all—that onetime teenage Leonard Cohen fan who goes by the name Bono, in a very rare solo foray away from the rest of U2.

Bill Flanagan remembers playing Cohen's version of "Hallelujah" for Bono on a homemade cassette during a drive in New Zealand in the fall of 1993, while he was on tour with the band reporting what would become the book *U2: At the End of the World*. As he mentions in the book, when the song reached the lines "You say I took the Name in vain; / I don't even know the name," Bono cracked up.

"His admiration for Leonard is tremendous," said Flanagan. "He sees him as a standard to shoot for, and one he still feels he hasn't matched."

"He's an extraordinary talent, and anyone who's interested in music has got to be interested in him," Bono would later tell MTV regarding Cohen. "Anyone who's interested in words needs to be interested in him. He's the original rapper, you know, if you're interested in hip-hop. He's a sexy man who made sexy music, who made music asking questions about God and girls and everything. Any question that I've wanted to ask, I've found in his mouth first."

In the film that ran as part of Cohen's induction into the Rock and Roll Hall of Fame, the U2 front man said, "I've been humbled and humiliated as a fan of Leonard Cohen's, particularly by the song 'Hallelujah.' "

Bono's "Hallelujah" on the *Tower of Song* album includes lyrics from both the *Various Positions* version of the song and the Cale/Buckley edit—five verses in all, reshuffled so that the "even though it all went wrong, / I'll stand before the Lord of Song" lines come in the middle and the "cold and broken Hallelujah" serves as the conclusion. It's an interesting sleight of hand, offering up a sense of hope and then snatching it away.

That alone might have made for a compelling take on the song—if it weren't for the fact that Bono's "Hallelujah" is, unfortunately, just awful. While there might seem to be no singer as well equipped to handle the song's balance of the earthly and the spiritual—whose own lyrics have frequently grappled with the same issues—for this recording, Bono opted for a lumbering trip-hop arrangement, produced by noted Scottish remixer Howie B. The singer mutters the verses over a limp beat (perhaps in tribute to his notion of Cohen as the "original rapper") and a darting trombone, with his voice leaping into a falsetto for the chorus that feels forced and passionless.

When Bono called from his home in Dublin to talk about "Hallelujah," his first words to me were, "I wasn't sure why I agreed to do this interview, but then I remembered that I needed to apologize to the world—I didn't just let myself down, or my parents, I let the whole school down.

"The lyric explains it best. There's the holy and the broken hallelujah, and mine was *definitely* the broken one. It was one of those moments—desperate, even wretched, and I was in desperate need of these words, and that's the only excuse. If you're that desperate to hear it, you sing it. It was a snapshot, a Polaroid, of a place I was in, but you really shouldn't go putting these things out when they're done in such a private way. Intimacy was the currency of the occasion."

U2 had been galvanized by the alternative and industrial rock movements of the early '90s, resulting in some of the band's finest work (the 1991 masterpiece *Achtung Baby* and the resultant Zoo TV tour) and some of its more daring but least convincing (the rapidly recorded follow-up *Zooropa* in 1993 and the *Original Soundtracks* ambient side project with producer Brian Eno, for which they billed themselves as the Passengers). Bono's rendition of "Hallelujah" seems very much of its moment, looking to electronic accompaniment for hip credibility and novelty rather than for what best served the song.

The generous reading is that at least Bono was trying for something different and challenging. It was too soon to compete with Buckley's version—Bono was an active champion of the young artist, once telling *Mojo* magazine that "Jeff Buckley was a pure drop in an ocean of noise"—and this reading, however flawed, does at least acknowledge the layered complexity of the song's images.

"I don't really remember being conscious of the Jeff

Buckley version at the time, though maybe that's why I did the whisper," said Bono. "If you can't take true flight and do his kind of Sufi singing, maybe stick to recitation. So I did it as beat poetry, with my fat-lady voice coming in in falsetto—it's remarkable I could even get up to that at the time.

"I think trip-hop was an interesting approach," he continued. "People would never think of Leonard Cohen in that way, even if it was more trip than hop, or we were tripping over the hop. I just remember wanting to fit in as much of the text as possible, really making it about the text. And I think it was reverent in all the right ways."

So let's be kind—where better to risk an experiment than on an overly sincere, second-time-around tribute album, anyway?

Around the release of the *Tower of Song* album, Robert Hilburn of the *Los Angeles Times* interviewed Cohen in his room at Mt. Baldy. "I stay here and do my work and help look after Roshi, who is the old teacher," Cohen said. "He's eighty-eight, and three or four of us are charged with doing that. Cooking is my contribution."

"The sixty-one-year-old songwriter and poet hasn't turned his back on the world," wrote Hilburn. "He frequently heads down the mountain to Los Angeles in his four-wheel-drive vehicle, either to visit an affiliated Zen center, to visit his daughter in the Mid-Wilshire area or meet with Kelley Lynch, his manager.

"Cohen has plenty of time here to devote to his writing. At present, he's working on an illustrated book of poems and songs for a future album. His workroom contains a primitive Macintosh computer and a synthesizer, tools for his music and his graphic art. There is also a radio in the room, but no CD or cassette player. He has to go out to his vehicle to play a CD."

Leonard Cohen might have removed himself from society, but even on the quiet mountaintop, he hadn't stopped working.

Meanwhile, Jeff Buckley spent much of 1995 and 1996 touring the world—making an endless loop around the United States, Europe, Australia, and Japan, from which various shows were recorded that have been released as albums and DVDs over the years. "Hallelujah" was his regular closing song, the emotional climax of his set every night, reducing his audiences to silence at the conclusion of an often frenzied evening.

Patti Smith invited Buckley to guest on her *Gone Again* album. During those sessions, he met guitarist Tom Verlaine, cofounder of the pioneering punk band Television, and asked Verlaine if he would produce his next album, which Buckley had decided would be called *My Sweetheart the Drunk*. In the middle of 1996, Buckley and his band started recording with Verlaine in New York, but the singer wasn't satisfied with the results they were getting.

In late 1996, Buckley did a "phantom solo tour" of the northeastern states, returning to the one-man approach and billed under a series of aliases. "There was a time in my life not too long ago when I could show up in a café and simply do what I do, make music, learn from performing my music, explore what it means to me, i.e., have fun while I irritate and/or entertain an audience who don't know me or what I am about," he wrote in an explanatory online Christmas message to his fans. "In this situation I have that precious and irreplaceable luxury of failure, of risk, of surrender. I worked very hard to get this kind of thing together, this work forum. I loved it and then I missed it when it disappeared. All I am doing is reclaiming it."

He gathered the band for another session with Verlaine in early 1997, but again was frustrated with how things were going. At the suggestion of his friend Dave Shouse from the scuzzy blues-punk band the Grifters, Buckley decided to try changing his surroundings: He moved to Memphis, Tennessee, rented a shotgun house, and set up shop at Easley McCain Recording studio, where such alt-rock royalty as Pavement and Sonic Youth had recently recorded. In February, Buckley and band did a third session with Verlaine but, still unhappy, the singer called Andy Wallace to discuss his taking over the production.

Buckley continued working on his new material the best way he knew, playing frequently at a downtown Memphis bar called Barrister's, even going so far as to take a weekly residency there, just like the old days at Sin-é. He was looking for a sound, and for a purpose—he often visited the Memphis Zoo and talked about volunteering there (there's now a plaque at the zoo commemorating him, purchased by Buckley fans around the world); he got around the city by bicycle; he let the grass grow at his house but meticulously sanded the floors. He was recording demos of the new songs on his own four-track recorder and sending them up to his band members in New York, who were scheduled to return to Memphis for rehearsals and recording sessions on May 29.

Penny Arcade, the former Andy Warhol superstar who had befriended Buckley during his early days in New York, wrote an online account of his final show at Barrister's on Monday, May 26. Tim Taylor, the lead singer in the cult favorite synth-punk band Brainiac, had died in a car crash. Buckley's first words on stage were "Dead, dead, dead, dead, dead, he's fucking dead, the guy from Brainiac is fucking dead. I want this to mean something to every fucking one of you."

Arcade writes that he "began to play 'Terminal Cancer,' a song that includes the line 'The world has eternal cancer'—'I guess that's how the guy from Brainiac felt,' he continued as he segued into 'Hallelujah' in requiem for Taylor." Later, when he performed "Corpus Christi Carol," a song he hadn't played live in over two years, Buckley said to the small crowd, "Is that how you like your rock heroes— dead?"

Three nights later, when the band arrived, Buckley and his friend and roadie Keith Foti were heading to the rehearsal studio and got lost. When the ever-impulsive singer figured out that they had ended up downtown, he suggested that they swing by the river—there was a spot in the Wolf River, a tributary of the Mississippi, where he had gone swimming, and he wanted to go back in. Though the water in the Wolf seems calm, natives know that its undercurrents can be deceptive.

Buckley waded in, still wearing his clothes and combat boots, and started singing Led Zeppelin's "Whole Lotta Love." At about nine-fifteen, after Jeff had been in the water for fifteen minutes, Foti saw a tugboat pass and called to Buckley to get out of the water. As the water got choppier, Foti got up to move his boom box so it wouldn't get splashed. When he turned back around, he didn't see Buckley.

Foti called the police, who began a search process. Boats, helicopters, and scuba divers all scoured the river and its banks, but after several hours, the efforts were called off. Six days later, on June 4, a riverboat passenger caught sight of something in the water. It was the body of Jeff Buckley.

The medical examiner at the University of Tennessee in Memphis announced that Buckley had tested negative for drugs, and that his blood alcohol level was insignificant, the equivalent of a glass of wine. The official cause of death was accidental drowning with "no evidence of other injuries." Buckley was thirty years old—two years older than his father had been when he died. His immense potential, his quest for transcendence through music, was stilled. But in ways no one could have anticipated, Jeff Buckley's popularity and influence would only expand in the years to come.

CHAPTER SIX

ollowing his passing, like those of other beautiful stars who died young, from James Dean to Tupac Shakur, Jeff Buckley's legend began to ascend. On June 7, 1997, just a few days after Buckley's body was found, U2 appeared at the second annual Tibetan Freedom benefit concert, organized by the Beastie Boys and held on New York City's Randall's Island. They closed their set with a churning version of "Please," a song from *Pop,* their most recent album, about the violence in Northern Ireland. This day, the band added a brief coda—a few delicate turns through the chorus of "Hallelujah," which stilled the crowd. Before walking off, Bono quietly said, "Jeff Buckley."

Numerous other friends and admirers—PJ Harvey, Chris Cornell, Rufus Wainwright, Aimee Mann, Glen Hansard—would also soon pay tribute to Buckley in song. Over time, *Grace* has sold more than three million copies worldwide, eventually earning gold sales status in the U.S. The album is platinum six times over in Australia. In Europe especially, a very dedicated Jeff Buckley cult began to arise. In 1998, Q magazine readers voted *Grace* the seventy-fifth greatest album of all time, and its standing would continue to rise as the years passed—as would the sense that this album, in truth a major commercial disappointment upon its release, had had a much bigger impact at the time than it actually did.

A batch of the demos and work tapes for the second album was released in 1998 under the title *Sketches for My Sweetheart the Drunk,* and a steady stream of unfinished recordings, outtakes, alternate takes, and live material would follow over the years. Nothing, though, would ever truly reveal where the promise of *Grace,* Buckley's one and only finished album, might have led. He is forever fixed as a wildly gifted, underappreciated artist beginning to bloom. We are left to imagine where his talents could have taken him, able only to project our own desires onto this blank screen.

After the publication of several books—most notably David Browne's dual biography of Tim and Jeff Buckley, *Dream Brother*—and the release of multiple documentaries about the singer, there has been a constant stream of rumors and struggles over the film rights to his story, which has been closely guarded by his mother, Mary Guibert. Brad Pitt has been among the Hollywood A-listers who fought unsuccessfully to assemble the Jeff Buckley story. (James Franco and *Twilight*'s Robert Pattinson are some of the other names that have been tossed around as possible on-screen Buckleys over the years.)

One film—*Greetings from Tim Buckley*, focusing primarily on Tim's story, and culminating with the appearance by Jeff (played by *Gossip Girl*'s Penn Badgley) at the St. Ann's show—enjoyed a well-received premiere at the Toronto International Film Festival in September 2012. In summer of 2011, it was announced that Jake Scott would be directing and Reeve Carney would be starring as Jeff in *Mystery White Boy*, the official biopic, sanctioned by Guibert; a year later, production had not started and Scott was replaced by Amy Berg, with reports that Carney may also be off the project.

No element of Buckley's history, though, has received more attention than his recording of "Hallelujah." The combination of the tragic young Buckley; Cohen, the revered songwriters' songwriter, recently endorsed by Bono, Reznor, and Cobain; and the haunting, mournful delivery of the prayer-like words proved irresistibly alluring for listeners.

It rippled out to the world, resonating as if Jeff Buckley had written his own epitaph. Years later, NPR said that the song "sounds almost ghostly—a fitting statement for a singer who's still finding new fans from beyond the grave." The association with a life cut too short further solidified the song as an expression of melancholy, rather than hard-won celebration.

After Buckley's death, "Hallelujah" took on an almost mythic stature. It was an insiders' secret for those who already knew about him, and an accessible pop song if it was functioning as an introduction. It now served as an elegy that went above and beyond actual words and music.

A decade after Buckley's death, at the 2007 Experience Music Project (EMP) conference in Seattle, an annual gathering of pop music academia, writer Michael Barthel presented a paper that was a landmark in "Hallelujah" studies. Titled "It Doesn't Matter Which You Heard: The Curious Cultural Journey of Leonard Cohen's 'Hallelujah,' " the presentation chronicled (complete with charts and graphs) the steady rise in visibility and popularity of the song. In the paper, Barthel described the transformation that occurred following Buckley's passing.

"However you come to the song, it's got an aura around it," he wrote. "If it's through Buckley, well, he's this beautiful dead boy with an apparently 'ethereal' voice, and he's singing this song that sounds like a long-ago thing. Cohen himself is distant enough at this point to be symbolically equivalent to an old blues guy: mysterious, wise, world-weary."

The bulk of Barthel's fascinating EMP presentation was an analysis of the cover versions and, especially, the film and television soundtrack uses of the song over the years to that point. An examination of the information that he assembled illustrates that starting in 1995—post-*Grace,* even prior to Buckley's death—the song begins turning up with increasing frequency. However misguided Bono's interpretation may have been, it seems like he had his finger on the pulse after all: In the second half of the 1990s, the flow of covers turns steady—there were three or four or five new versions a year, each year. Most of these early versions came from Europe; singers in Denmark, Spain, Finland, Germany, Holland, and the Czech Republic all recorded "Hallelujah" during this time.

Even more notable, however, is the development that would most dramatically define the standing of "Hallelujah" in the pop universe—the first uses of the song on movie soundtracks. Though these appearances did follow the release of *Grace,* they didn't initially focus on Buckley's recording. John Cale's version appears under the end credits in the 1996 film *Basquiat,* painter Julian Schnabel's dream-like biography of the graffiti writer–turned–art star Jean-Michel Basquiat. (Given Basquiat's connection to Andy Warhol, played by David Bowie in the movie, and Warhol's relationship to the Velvet Underground, Cale's former band, this choice was a subtle but significant one.)

"Hallelujah" then turned up in a few Australian movies over the next several years. Though Buckley had—and has to this day—an especially passionate fan base in Australia, these soundtracks utilized versions by local singers. Simon

Austin, a former member of the popular band Frente!, sang it for *River Street,* and jazz trumpeter Vince Jones performed it for *Siam Sunset.*

In 1999, Sheryl Crow sang "Hallelujah" on the public television music series *Sessions at West 54th.* Barefoot and perched on a tall bar stool, she performed a sped-up rendition of Buckley's arrangement. Crow adds a nice, finger-picked guitar solo before the final verse, but she stumbles in the first few lines ("It goes like this: the fourth, the fifth / the minor third and the major fifth," she sings, taking the lesson in harmony a step too far—obviously the song was not yet so familiar that these lines were permanently burned into every young singer-songwriter's brain).

A pattern was being established. With all of these covers and soundtracks, every year saw a half-dozen or so new impressions of "Hallelujah." Immediately obvious, too, was that its use behind dramatic scenes was effective: The mood and melody, the backstory, the chorus, and (less crucial, or at least selectively important) the lyrics added a powerful emotional jolt to a scripted scene. Directors and music supervisors discovered that, as with all good soundtrack songs, "Hallelujah" provided a shortcut—to feelings of contemplation, loss, solitude—in just a few bars.

As Leonard Cohen remained in isolation, a second collection of his best-known songs (it's a bit hard to say "Greatest Hits" for an artist who has never actually had any hits),

titled *More Best of Leonard Cohen,* came out in October 1997.
Though most of the set was drawn from *I'm Your Man* and *The
Future,* plus two previously unreleased tracks, this time "Hallelujah" was most certainly included—the *Cohen Live* version,
in the construction that inspired John Cale, closer in spirit to
the Jeff Buckley cover that was now the song's calling card.

From the monastery atop Mt. Baldy, Leonard Cohen might
have wondered why more and more royalty checks started
coming in from around the world for this one composition—
though, as we'll soon see, perhaps he wasn't actually informed
of this development. It's unclear how aware he was of the Jeff
Buckley cover. Bill Flanagan recalls speaking to Cohen a number of years ago and bringing up Buckley's "Hallelujah."

"I got the impression that Leonard was actually not that
familiar with it—like he might have heard Jeff's version, but
he didn't know that much about it," said Flanagan. "I remember he asked me, 'He was the son of Tim Buckley. Did
he die the same way?' "

In 1999, Cohen came down the mountain and quietly
returned to his home in Los Angeles. He had already begun
e-mailing poems, drawings, and new song lyrics to the
Leonard Cohen Files fan website (these writings can still be
found on the site, in a section titled "The Blackening Pages").
Whether or not the rise of "Hallelujah" entered into his thinking, Cohen's spiritual retreat had ended, and he was creating
for an audience again, in time for a new millennium to begin.

CHAPTER SEVEN

In 2001, "Hallelujah" was seventeen years old—almost a full generation in the real world, and thoroughly ancient in the pop universe. Its author, now nearing seventy years old, had barely been seen in public for almost a decade.

Meanwhile, since the advent of the Napster peer-to-peer file-sharing service in 1999, the music business was being turned upside down. Though the year 2000, driven by the teen-pop bonanza, represented a high-water mark for record sales—no fewer than five albums that year sold over a million copies during their first week of release—the digital revolution would soon cause the bottom to fall out of the industry, and the economics and culture of music were in the midst of a radical recalibration.

Yet, in 2001, "Hallelujah" would undergo a shift, in which it would no longer just be a song but also become a phenomenon, and would illustrate the power and impact that a piece of music could still have in the twenty-first century, however listeners were buying or consuming recordings. Several events—silly events alongside incomprehensibly tragic events—occurred within a few months of each other that altered the stature and meaning of this song forever.

In 1991, Steven Spielberg had bought the rights to a new children's book by William Steig titled *Shrek!*, the story of a loner ogre who finds true love. For years, the project languished in development hell. When the DreamWorks studio was founded, the story was brought to Jeffrey Katzenberg's attention; in the mid-nineties, he acquired the rights and put the film into production.

From the very beginning, the making of *Shrek* was fraught with complications. Codirector Andrew Adamson immediately clashed with Katzenberg over how far the movie could push its humor into adult territory. *Saturday Night Live*'s latest breakout star, Chris Farley, had recorded almost all of his dialogue as the voice of Shrek when he died in December 1997. Farley's *SNL* predecessor Mike Myers, now a movie star thanks to *Wayne's World* and *Austin Powers*, was given the role, but he insisted on a complete rewrite.

After recording his entire part, Myers asked to rerecord all of his lines in a Scottish accent that reminded him of his parents telling him bedtime stories. Meanwhile, Janeane Garofalo, who had been cast as the voice of Princess Fiona opposite Farley, was abruptly fired ("I was never told why," she said later. "I assume because I sound like a man sometimes?"), and ultimately replaced by Cameron Diaz.

"The movie was very much a bastard child of the studio," said Adamson from Australia when I spoke to him over the phone. "But it led to people being bolder and braver, being willing to take more chances and just go with it."

One way in which the filmmakers took some risks was in the prominent inclusion of rock and pop songs—not the usual accompaniment to a fairy tale. Songs by Smash Mouth (whose slots opening and closing the film may be the greatest legacy in their largely forgettable career), Joan Jett, and the Proclaimers were given significant placements in *Shrek*.

The most surprising musical selection came at the movie's emotional climax. Shrek has rescued Princess Fiona from her isolated castle and is on his way to deliver her to her future husband, Lord Farquaad. Their feelings for each other are growing when Shrek misinterprets part of an overheard conversation and thinks Fiona is disgusted with him. When morning comes, Shrek has brought Lord Farquaad and his troops to collect Fiona. The couple heads for his castle, while a devastated Shrek retreats alone to his now-vacated swamp.

A montage follows, with scenes of Shrek pining for Fiona while the princess joylessly prepares for her wedding. Behind this action, music plays: John Cale singing an abbreviated, three-verse "Hallelujah."

And somehow, as weird and unlikely as the choice may be, it works—the sorrowful but unsentimental tone fits the sophistication of a cartoon that features fart jokes and not-so-subtle sexual innuendo. A few of the lines ("I used to live alone before I knew you," "love is not a victory march") even manage to line up nicely with the narrative. With words courtesy of the Prince of Bummers, and vocals by the man who snarled "Fear Is a Man's Best Friend," the musical moment proved unforgettable.

The scene served as evidence once and for all that this song held an irresistible emotional impact that transcended generations. Even for the adults in the audience, who might find more irony in the scene than their kids, the song had to live or die on the feeling it presented—at the time, very few viewers would have been familiar with "Hallelujah" in any of its extant recordings, so it couldn't rely on associations the listeners might already have had with the song in order to generate a reaction.

Codirector Adamson was a longtime Cohen fan, but even he had been unaware of "Hallelujah" until he heard Cale's version on the *Basquiat* soundtrack. "I came from outside the animation world, and the movie was very much under the radar at DreamWorks," he said. "At the early stages of *Shrek,* we were temping it with music by Tom Waits and a number of other people I just liked—definitely not what you would expect in an animated film—and people started reacting to that. We would sit in a room with our favorite songs and start putting them up against different scenes."

Adamson's codirector, Vicky Jenson, had the Cale recording in her collection, so they tried it in the separation scene, and then also considered the versions by Cohen and Buckley. "For that scene, the Cale version just seemed to have the right feel of longing," said Adamson. "I actually thought Buckley's might have a better feeling given the tone, but it didn't—it's amazing, it's such a reinterpretation with a more contemporary feel, but it still wasn't better.

"The song came at a moment of emotional irony, taking something that's a celebration and playing against itself. It's a sad moment, after he's been through this huge experience, with a sense of how it's better to have loved and lost."

An even bigger shock was the positive response that the directors received to their unconventional choice. "People reacted immediately, which, to be honest, surprised me," said Adamson. "I expected that the studio would push me to do something more popular, which they often do, but the emotion really outweighed the expectation.

"I think there's a sense that Leonard Cohen songs are for grown-ups, for people who are melancholy, yet if they're presented to an audience in a different way, they react to the emotion. This was Shrek's voice, his path it was tracking. It became his song, and it didn't carry that baggage." Listeners encountering the song cold, in such an unexpected context, didn't have to get past the fact that it was written by a "difficult" adult artist; they just responded to the feelings they got from the music.

In May of 2001, after almost five years of production, *Shrek* was released. The movie would become the third-highest-grossing film of the year, and go on to take in almost $500 million worldwide and win the first-ever Academy Award for Best Animated Feature. The franchise flourished over the following decade, spawning three sequels, several television specials, a Broadway musical, and numerous video games.

Yet when *Shrek* fans young and old picked up the soundtrack album—which reached the Top 30 of the U.S. album charts, and was nominated for a Grammy Award— "Hallelujah" was there, but John Cale was nowhere to be found. In the name of corporate synergy, it was decided that if the soundtrack to a DreamWorks movie was coming out on DreamWorks Records, it should include only artists who were signed to the label. So it came to pass that an acclaimed, widely buzzed-about young singer named Rufus Wainwright performed the song on the album, adding yet another rendition to the "Hallelujah" canon—a version that would become one of the most popular of all.

Though Wainwright—who was raised in Cohen's native

Montreal—was well aware of Cohen's work, and moved in many of the same New York City circles as Jeff Buckley (and, like Buckley, had a father who was a well-respected singer-songwriter, Loudon Wainwright III), he claims that he was not really familiar with "Hallelujah" at the time. "Initially, I was never really attuned to its significance," he said over a vegetarian Chinese lunch at a midtown Manhattan recording studio, during a break from work on his 2012 album *Out of the Game*. "Mainly because when I covered it, a) I hadn't heard the Jeff Buckley version, and b) even at that point, his was the only real substantial one. Even Leonard's was considered kind of a throwaway track. I learned it from the John Cale version, which is very beautiful."

Wainwright laughed as he recounted how his own jealousy had prevented him from paying much attention to Buckley in the '90s. "We'd kind of been in the same environment for a while. All those places like Sin-é and Fez, I would bring my demos by and they would always refuse them, and Jeff would be up there cavorting. So I was very jealous and spiteful. And then, lo and behold, he died—and then, of course, listening to his music after the fact, he was incredibly talented."

He recalled the epiphany that later enabled him to make peace with Buckley's memory, and with his performance of "Hallelujah." "I was in Montreal," said Wainwright, "and

I was alone and probably on something. I put his version of the song on, and it was this kind of cosmic communion. It kind of hit me how great he was, and how fabulous the song is, and how foolish I had been for being so petty and having this jealousy thing with him. I really felt like he was visiting me cosmically, in some strange way."

In 2004, Wainwright included the song "Memphis Skyline" on his *Want Two* album, the bulk of which was recorded at Bearsville Studios. It was his tribute to Jeff Buckley. "Always hated him for the way he looked / in the gaslight of the morning," he sang. "Then came Hallelujah, sounding like mad Ophelia / for me in my room living." He sometimes performed the song immediately following "Hallelujah" in concert.

Maybe it was his initial resistance to Buckley, though, that allowed Wainwright's "Hallelujah" to find its own path. The arrangement as included on the *Shrek* soundtrack is clearly modeled on Cale's solo piano approach, but Wainwright is able to find a mood that reveals yet another facet of the song, more a pure celebration of the melody than the struggle present in the previous renditions. "I do a pretty good version of it," Wainwright said with typical cheekiness. "It has that emotional quality, but I don't belabor that fact; I don't wallow in a lot of that stuff. I go through it in a simple way, and it's a little more streamlined." With the most conventionally grand singing voice of the "Hallelujah" interpreters to date, Wainwright puts more focus on the sound and flow of the song than on the complexities of its meaning.

"If I had to go out there and sing it half as fast, and always have to pretend like I'm about to kill myself, then that would be another story. But I can do it in a nice, quick way where it's more intimate, almost laissez-faire in a sense, which I think works well with the song."

While Wainwright's inclusion on the *Shrek* record may have been a corporate decision, ultimately it proved to be one more lucky break in the "Hallelujah" saga. Cale's dolorous, bitter-edged version lent gravity and emotional weight to the scene in the movie, but Wainwright's lighter, melodic take was more accessible standing on its own, easier listening for the kids around the world playing and replaying the soundtrack. (Andrew Adamson said that the filmmakers did try the Wainwright recording with the scene, but still preferred Cale's version.)

"*Shrek* launched into popular culture so quickly, in a way I never expected," said Adamson. "I had no sense of how much the characters would become part of popular culture. Suddenly you had six-year-old kids singing 'Hallelujah'—it definitely reached a very different audience. But kids just accept it as the song from *Shrek*."

Indeed, for millions of millennial kids, "Hallelujah" had simply become "the *Shrek* song;" a quick skim through the countless homemade YouTube videos of the song reveals numerous clips listed with this subtitle. It started to enter the realm of summer-camp sing-alongs and school talent shows. Introduced in the context of the movie, which established its emotional heft, then reinforced with the easier-to-swallow soundtrack version, the basic core of the song (if not its every nuance) was resonating more and more universally.

But even as "Hallelujah" was becoming permanently associated with a giant green cartoon character, history had other plans for Leonard Cohen's composition, and for Jeff Buckley's voice.

When terrorists hijacked four airplanes on September 11, 2001, and killed nearly three thousand people, there was no time to prepare a reaction. During the hours and days that followed the destruction of that morning, people were struggling for ways to process or address the tragedy. The media scrambled to make sense of senseless events, improvising what coverage was necessary, what statements were appropriate.

Around the world, viewers were glued to their television sets, looking for information or explanation. And these same issues had to be addressed at the entertainment broadcasters—maybe the stakes weren't as high for MTV as they were for CNN, but the network still had choices to

make about how best to serve its viewers at such an unprecedented moment of crisis for the United States.

Within the music community, songs were being written, benefit concerts were being organized, lyrics and video
images were taking on new overtones. Radio titan Clear
Channel Communications sent out a controversial memo
to its stations pointing out songs with "questionable lyrics"
for this charged moment, which ranged from the Gap Band's
"You Dropped a Bomb on Me" and the Bangles' "Walk Like
an Egyptian" to the songs of Rage Against the Machine and
John Lennon's "Imagine."

Fred Graver was an executive producer for VH1 at the
time. The network was winnowing down its video playlist
in the aftermath of the attacks: He remembers looking at
his screen and seeing the clip for the Goo Goo Dolls' hit
"Iris," from the film *City of Angels,* and watching a shot of
Nicolas Cage jumping from a building and realizing that
it was another video that had to be dropped. As soon as
possible, he wanted to make sure to get a special tribute of
some kind on the air, honoring the victims and the rescue
workers.

"There were two bits of tape that we had in the twenty-
four hours after," he said. "There was a crew shooting for
a producer named Steve Rosenbaum, who ran something
called City TV. They picked up their cameras when the

planes hit, and while everybody was running out of the towers, they ran in—it was devastating, all the dust and ruins and people running. An editor placed a song that the band Live had put up ["Overcome"] behind that. And then our news crew just went around to places like Union Square, everywhere people were gathering. So we took all this footage and cut it down to a three- or four-minute thing."

Scattered VH1 staffers who were in the office saw the clip, and some weighed in with thoughts on what music should accompany this footage. Sarah Lewitinn was working at the time as the assistant to Michael Hirschorn, head of the network's news operations. More widely known by her online pseudonym "Ultragrrrl," Lewitinn would soon begin a full-time juggling act as a record producer, party promoter, DJ, and blogger, and in 2006, be named one of the most influential people in music by *New York* magazine. (She started her career as an intern at *Spin* magazine while I was the publication's editor in chief.) According to Graver, "it was Sarah who said, 'What you want here is Jeff Buckley's version of "Hallelujah." ' "

Asked if she remembers making this suggestion, Lewitinn said that she has mostly erased the days around September 11 from her memory. To jog her recollections, she wrote to her brother Lawrence to see what he could remember from that traumatic time. She then sent me the following message, which is slightly edited and with IM names redacted:

lawrence: I remember it well

lawrence: you suggested it at a meeting

lawrence: VH1 people acted confused

lawrence: they wanted to use something else

lawrence: something lame

lawrence: You thought the Buckley version was good

ultragrrrl: the only thing i remember from that
    time was watching the buildings fall. I don't even
    remember the VH1 meetings.

lawrence: You thought the way it was sung was the
    perfect tempo

lawrence: Plus, Buckley was a tragic person himself

lawrence: At the time, no one really knew the
    Buckley version at VH1, either

lawrence: You did because you were a fan.

lawrence: Wait, does that mean it's your fault that
    song is now on every season of *American Idol*?

ultragrrrl: yup

lawrence: jerk

"Lots of people did not know it," confirmed Graver. "I'm a huge Leonard Cohen fan, but I didn't know Buckley's version. But that long, languorous guitar lead-in, those pliant, beautiful notes—it was perfect. The song is open to a lot of interpretations, but Buckley's sounds like it comes from one person's broken heart, broken spirit—it drives straight through.

"If you really listen to the song, it doesn't quite fit what was happening," Graver pointed out. "But if you talk to a songwriter, or even someone making TV, they'll say, 'I create an emotion, people react to it, they rarely hear the whole thing.' And the reaction was instantaneous. We basically turned the network over completely to tributes, videos that fit the mood, for the entire weekend."

"I came into the office on September 12 and Fred said, 'Come take a look at this,' " said Bill Flanagan. "It had just been delivered to him, and we watched footage of the smoking World Trade Center over 'Hallelujah' by Jeff Buckley. He said, 'We're going to put this right into rotation; we're going to play it every hour.' And I said, 'You know, that's not really what the song is about.' And he said, 'It doesn't matter.'

"And he was right: It didn't matter. The song had become something—it had already become something, but I think that was the first time that I realized that it really wasn't a song about regret and the waning of sexual desire and all that stuff. It had become a spiritual."

Heard against the horrifying, bewildering, inspiring footage of the rubble, of the rescue workers and the vigils, of the tears and rage, the yearning physicality of Jeff Buckley's "Hallelujah" had precisely the necessary tone for the moment—the feelings of love and loss, of mystic confusion that didn't surrender to despair.

The video played constantly on VH1 in the days that

followed September 11. In his 2010 novel *Evening's Empire*, Flanagan wrote of the days after the attacks that "Leonard Cohen's 'Hallelujah' in all its incarnations became an anthem that month."

Whether serving as consolation for a lovesick ogre or as a balm for a scarred and grieving nation, over the course of a few months "Hallelujah" had solidified its place as a modern-day hymn. It felt like something larger now, a connection to a broader kind of spirituality than the personal, one-on-one relationships its interpreters had been expressing; that chorus and its calming melody had been thrust even more front and center. Millions of new listeners, from multiple generations, were introduced to the song, with indelible feelings attached to it. What had been an insiders' favorite for music aficionados now belonged to the general public in a way that very few songs ever have. As Fred Graver said, referencing Robert Frost, "A poem is going to get up and walk away and it's not yours anymore."

On top of the surge in attention that "Hallelujah" was receiving in 2001, that October Leonard Cohen returned from seven years of self-imposed exile with the acclaimed *Ten New Songs* album. The record was a triumphant if understated effort from an artist who had seemed as if he might fade into the realm of pure myth. Praise from such outlets as the indie rock hub Pitchfork.com proved Cohen's hipster cred was still thriving.

Since it came out, coincidentally, just a few weeks after Bob Dylan's *Love and Theft* album (which had a street date of September 11, lending an eerie weight to his end-of-days lines about "Sky full of fire, pain pourin' down" or "Coffins droppin' in the street / Like balloons made out of lead"), the two songwriting giants were sometimes even reviewed together—a boost in visibility and reputation that certainly helped Cohen's profile.

Recorded in collaboration with backup singer Sharon Robinson, *Ten New Songs* marked a new sense of sparseness and austerity for Cohen, with minimal music settings and a voice that rarely rose above a murmur. Recorded at Cohen and Robinson's home studios, the basic synthesizer arrangements may have sounded "like an orchestra" to Cohen, though for some they registered as little more than a monotone; in an excellent aside, Mireille Silcott wrote in the Canadian magazine *Saturday Night* that a friend of hers said that the album "sounds like a guy in the subway with a keyboard who decided to burn a CD."

The lyrics were reflective and weary, less spiky and less grand than those on *I'm Your Man* and *The Future*—perhaps not surprising for a man who had spent most of the previous decade in a Zen monastery. Cohen said in interviews that a lengthy depression had lifted two years earlier, accounting for the calm and clarity of the new lyrics. Some of the *Ten New Songs* would be covered by artists from Eric Burdon of the Animals to the jam band Widespread Panic, and a few years later, our old friend John Cale would select the album's "Alexandra Leaving" as one of his "Desert Island Discs" for the BBC.

Whether it was a direct result of the nascent "Hallelujah"-mania or not, *Ten New Songs* was also a commercial peak for Cohen. He returned to the U.S. album charts (a relatively modest Number 143, but still) for the first time since 1973. The disc went Top Five in Israel and Italy, hit Number Four in Canada, and reached Number One in Norway, Denmark, and Poland.

Cohen did quite a bit of press around the release of the album. Apparently, though, it was still too soon after the *Shrek* and VH1 usages of the song to feel the impact, because only a few interviews so much as made mention of "Hallelujah."

At least one writer picked up on the rumblings, though. In a November 18, 2001, feature in the *Denver Post,* Steven Rosen recounted "Leonard Cohen's Unlikely Debt to a Famous Green Ogre," noting that "Hallelujah" had been "taking on a life apart from Cohen's recording," walking through the song's history via Dylan, Cale, Buckley, and September 11. "For *Shrek*'s help in making this song a recognizable contemporary standard, one can only say Hallelujah!" wrote Rosen. Cohen declined an interview request for the story.

Though most cultural observers hadn't noticed it yet, everything was now in place for "Hallelujah" to sweep through the pop landscape. It was a song that had multiple strong, emotional connections with millions of listeners. Its mood was both fixed and malleable, universal and specific. It was familiar enough to resonate, obscure enough to remain cool. Though its most celebrated performer was gone forever, its mysterious creator had come back to the spotlight just in time.

After 2001, whether it signified an individual's solitude (human or monster or otherwise) or a population in mourning, "Hallelujah"—now far removed from Leonard Cohen's initial, "rather joyous" intent—was established as the definitive representation of sadness for a new generation.

CHAPTER EIGHT

Sony/ATV Music Publishing is the publishing company for the songs of both Leonard Cohen and Jeff Buckley. The company's job is to monitor the uses of the compositions in its catalogue and to find new placements and possibilities for these songs—and if the media had not fully caught on to what was happening with "Hallelujah," the publishers certainly knew, and they realized that an opportunity like this was too good to pass up. They made sure that "Hallelujah" was in front of the executives who put together soundtracks and musical scores for movies and television. They were obviously savvy about their work, but even they couldn't fully anticipate what was coming.

In 2001, John Cale's version showed up in the first season of Zach Braff's medical sitcom, *Scrubs*. The next year, Buckley's version of "Hallelujah" appeared in an episode of *The West Wing,* and twice in the first season of the teen soap opera *The O.C.*—including a highly visible slot at the conclusion of the show's season finale.

Alexandra Patsavas is one of the most prominent music supervisors in film and television. She played a crucial role in helping to make placements in TV dramas a powerful tool in promoting and breaking new songs and artists, especially during a time of radio consolidation and the de-emphasizing of music video at the TV music channels. She has worked on such shows as *Grey's Anatomy* and *Gossip Girl,* and films including the *Twilight* series.

"The song has so much depth on its own that it's really important it be paired with a very emotional scene or a very pivotal scene, because it can lend so much depth," Patsavas has said, explaining her multiple uses of "Hallelujah" on *The O.C.* "It's not something you would sync lightly—sync means to pair with picture, synchronize—because of how much more it could make a scene *feel*."

According to Michael Barthel's EMP paper, the song's use in movie and TV soundtracks went from one appearance in 2002 to five in 2003 to seven in 2004. Shows such as *The L Word* and *House* continued to keep the song in network rotation (usually Buckley's recording, occasionally Cale's or Wainwright's, and never one of the Cohen versions), even after all of these other placements started piling up. Apparently, the song's impact was rising as it became more familiar, rather than becoming dulled through increased exposure.

" 'Hallelujah' can be joyous or bittersweet, depending on what part of it you use," said Sony/ATV's Kathy Coleman. "It's one of those rare songs that the more it gets used, the more people want to use it."

As late as 2004—which was actually the year that the number of soundtrack placements reached its peak—*Time* magazine took note of the "Hallelujah" explosion; "because it covers so much emotional ground and is not (yet) a painfully obvious choice," the story said, "it has become the go-to track whenever a TV show wants to create instant mood."

Writer Josh Tyrangiel added that "some shows use just a snippet, but *The West Wing* and *Without a Trace* let it play for minutes over their season finales, a tacit admission that neither the writers nor the actors could convey their characters' emotions as well as Buckley."

But make no mistake: While it is absolutely correct that the song "can be joyous or bittersweet" and that "it covers so much emotional ground," its use on virtually all of these soundtracks was to do one thing—to provide the feeling of people being sad.

On *The West Wing,* "Hallelujah" plays when the press secretary's secret service guard (and love interest) is gunned down trying to stop a robbery at a convenience store while the president and his staff are attending an opera. In the final moments of an *ER* season finale, it plays under cuts between scenes from multiple pain-ridden story lines: Sarah's grandparents driving onto the highway, taking her away from Gates, who has lost his custody battle; Ray being taken home in an ambulance with his mother, after having his legs amputated; and Neela attending an antiwar rally that later erupts into chaos.

This point was the crux of Barthel's EMP presentation and, complete with video examples, he made an airtight case for the codification of "Hallelujah," its compression into a single mood. "What's fascinating about all this is not simply the song's ubiquity on TV dramas—it's that it's used in the exact same way every time," he said. "Songs can be used sincerely, ironically, as background shading, as subtle comment, as product placement. But 'Hallelujah' always appears as people are being sad, quietly sitting and staring into space or ostentatiously crying, and always as a way of tying together the sadness of different characters in different places. In short, it's always used as part of a 'sad montage.' "

Barthel compared the use of the song to the "emotional shorthand" of a silent film actress holding the back of her hand to her forehead to express despair. But like that gesture, the song is indirect, never explicitly proclaiming its sense of sorrow. The ambiguity of Cohen's words can "both reinforce and counterpoint" the feeling of the scene.

The ultimate effect, he argues, is that the repeated use of "Hallelujah" for identical dramatic purpose has "erased the line-by-line, verse-by-verse meaning and replaced it with an overall feeling of sadness. You hear those opening chords now and the words hardly matter. The visual emotions it was used to counterpoint have overtaken the lyrical content." With the benefit of hindsight, maybe his point is a little overstated, but it's true at heart—during this phase, the association with these tragic dramatic scenes was so strong, and the repetitions so frequent, that it was difficult to hear the actual words and meaning of the song itself.

As each of these popular shows introduced the song to millions more listeners, these impressions accrued and continually fed on one another. Soon, the song had truly become a fully functional narrative device, cueing up a response from viewers as instantaneously as "Walking on Sunshine" represents carefree joy or "Born to Be Wild" signifies badass abandon.

The money generated from these usages was not insignificant, either: A rough estimate of the price for a television placement is somewhere in the mid five figures. If we assume a $50,000 fee, that sum is then carved up into two halves, for the recording and for the songwriter. Each $25,000 would then be divided again, between the artist and the record company, and between the writer and his publisher. For each licensing of Jeff Buckley's "Hallelujah," then, Buckley's estate, Cohen, Columbia Records, and Sony/ATV Publishing each walk away with $12,500—which can start to add up over dozens of placements.

Following the explosion in the use of (mostly) Buckley's performance of the song, the next advance in soundtrack placement involved generating new versions to be employed as on-screen accompaniment. After *The O.C.* utilized Buckley in its first season finale in 2004, Patsavas put British singer Imogen Heap's "Hide and Seek" under the climax of the second season. For the third season, the show went full-on high-concept and asked Heap to record a new "Hallelujah" for the closing episode.

"There was so much pressure on the song, and I was kind of terrified at the thought of having to do it," said Heap. "I worried that I wasn't doing it for the right reasons, plus I was in the middle of touring, really busy, so I had to find a way to carve out the time and space to make it something meaningful.

"I had actually just sent an e-mail to the show saying I was sorry, but I wouldn't be able to give this the time it requires. I was in the shower and feeling a bit sad about it, and I started singing it and thought, 'Why don't I just do it this way—do it a cappella, with no music or production, as if I were singing in the shower?' So I got out and I sent them another e-mail back, saying what if I do this, but not have it totally empty, maybe go on my balcony and record the sound of the city, the sound of London, around it. Then I had found the connection that I needed, and I created this scene, up in a council flat."

Heap, who first came to the public's attention through a different soundtrack placement—when Zach Braff used a song by her band, Frou Frou, on the influential soundtrack to the 2004 movie *Garden State*—expected that it would be easy to knock out a solo vocal of the two verses she chose from "Hallelujah," but it ended up taking a few days to get it right.

"I'd never done anything like that, where I take on a character and then let it speak for itself," she said. "In the scene, this character, Marissa, had been killed, and there were images of the funeral. I never actually saw the scene, but they described it to me. I thought these were the right verses, though some people were annoyed at me for not doing the whole track. It was a good challenge, and an emotional experience."

Casting Heap to record the song was a bit of a stunt, but the placement seemed to work well for the show's fans (and lives on, courtesy of YouTube). Music supervisor Patsavas said that "Imogen's voice, the use of 'Hallelujah,' and then those things together combined to make a special sort of extra-*O.C.* ending."

Kate Voegele's relationship to "Hallelujah" was very different from Imogen Heap's when she performed the song on *One Tree Hill*, another teen drama. Voegele, a young musician and actress, played the role of singer-songwriter Mia Catalano on the series. She first heard the song when she was in high school in Ohio and grew "obsessed" with Jeff Buckley, and taught herself to play it during her freshman year at college.

"My friends were all like, 'You've got to play that song out!' " she said, "and I was like, 'No, I can't touch it—it's an untouchable song.' But eventually I decided to say screw it and do it anyways. People were always receptive and cool at my shows, but there were always a bunch of drunk college kids, and when I played that song, I remember it freaked me out how quiet everybody was."

Voegele left Miami University after two years, made her first record, and started touring on a package with several other singer-songwriters. "Before one show I was going through my set list," she recalls, "and I was like, 'Oh, I think I'm going to play "Hallelujah." ' And one of the other singers, Cary Brothers, was like, 'No, you're not. Don't touch that song. Nobody can touch that song.' I was young, I was nervous, I wanted to take everybody's advice. But I got up there, and I looked out at the crowd and I was like, 'You know what? I'm just going to play this song.'

"I told the story onstage and said, 'Listen, I don't know if everybody's going to hate on me for this, because I know that a lot of hipster people feel like this song is overdone, but I think it's so beautiful and it deserves to be heard, so I'm going to play it.' I sold so many records that night—I didn't even have the song on my record, but just because I won people over with that song. I teased Cary about it for the rest of the tour, and I played it every night."

Soon, she was cast in her recurring role on *One Tree Hill*, which featured several of her own compositions, sung in character, through the show's fifth season in 2008. As the season reached its end, though, and the dramatic stakes were getting higher, it was time to pull out the big guns and have Voegele sing "Hallelujah." The penultimate episode's waning moments were given over to almost a full five minutes of the song—all five of the Cale/Buckley version's verses—as scenes jumped across story arcs from a fight at a high school basketball game to a newborn intensive care nursery.

"What's so beautiful about 'Hallelujah' is that it's a song for when you don't have answers," Voegele said.

Released as a single, her "Hallelujah" actually achieved something that none of the previous versions had—it reached the pop charts, climbing to Number 68 in the U.S. and Number 53 in the UK. Voegele's performance also remains one of the most popular on YouTube, where it has garnered over fifteen million total views.

"The show essentially did for me what radio might do for an artist with a big song," she said. "But it was a cool feeling that people trusted me with it."

Concurrent with the rising popularity of "Hallelujah" as a soundtrack selection, more and more singers were recording their own versions of the song. In 2001, five covers of the song were released; the next year, that number almost tripled, to fourteen covers; and in 2004, no fewer than twenty different versions came out.

This initial wave of covers—most of them, to be accurate, were covers of Buckley's cover of Cale's cover—came from artists who were still emerging or not very well-known. The song still felt like a discovery, a gem that could be unearthed and used to lend gravitas and taste to a developing career. This was the phase when, as Bill Flanagan recalls, "every time you walked into a showcase at the South by Southwest festival it was like, 'Here's two songs I wrote and "Hallelujah." ' " In her early days breaking into the business, Brandi Carlile remembers playing at the Hotel Café, a premier showcase spot for young singer-songwriters in Los Angeles, and seeing a sign taped to the wall behind the soundboard that read, PLEASE DO NOT SING "HALLELUJAH."

Some of the artists who tackled the song during the first few years of the decade were the young English band Starsailor (named, probably not coincidentally, after a Tim Buckley song), jazz-pop trumpeter Chris Botti, and Canadian singer-songwriter Allison Crowe, whose version demonstrated surprising longevity and also became a YouTube favorite. A close look at the staggering and ever-expanding list of covers as documented on the Leonard Cohen Files website also reveals a bunch of recordings from Scandinavia and Germany.

Another Canadian, alt-country singer Fred Eaglesmith, recorded the song for a Country Music Television Christmas record. Oversize guitar shredder Popa Chubby, better known for Jimi Hendrix covers and other blues-bar favorites, added a spiky version of "Hallelujah" to his set, where it remains to this day.

Acclaimed singer-songwriter Regina Spektor chose the song as her contribution to a concert for the Jewish Heritage Festival in September 2005, an annual event at which Jewish performers sing material written by Jewish composers. Russian-born, Bronx-raised Spektor first heard *Grace* when she was in college, and assumed that Buckley had written the song. ("Now I just get annoyed at those people, but I was one of those people!" she said.) When she first heard Cohen's recording at a friend's apartment, she asked, "Why did he add all this other stuff?"

As she came to learn more about Cohen's work, though, Spektor became entranced. "The production on his records reminds me of old Russian movies," she said. "It feels like you're in a restaurant in the '70s—the decade has a melancholy vibe to it, a certain color scheme."

She thought that "Hallelujah" seemed like the appropriate choice for a celebration of Jewish art. "Cohen writes a lot with biblical symbolism at the forefront of his mind," she said. "Having gone to yeshiva and studied those stories, I know that all the biblical things are so unique lyrically, and he uses them so freely, but you don't have to know the stories to appreciate the song."

Spektor relates the Bible stories "Hallelujah" invokes not only to the characters and language, but also to the song's sense of searching and ambivalence. "The Torah is used to help translate emotions—it's like a compass for getting through life. For something from 500 B.C., it's pretty fucking modern," she said. "However literal or philosophical, it's still a blueprint for something, and he's using those stories and traditional Jewish history. The king was conflicted, so he's using that for his own blueprint."

Spektor was twenty-five when she performed the song; she had only recently made the leap from the downtown "anti-folk" scene to a major label, and her commercial breakthrough, the Top 20 *Begin to Hope* album, wouldn't be released until the next year. Her performance of "Hallelujah" is fascinating—her voice seems tentative, almost quizzical at times, then leaping into celebratory release. Accompanied only by a cello, she seems to be feeling her way through the song, and as an almost inadvertent result, attains some of the triumphant confusion that Cohen intended.

Five years later, with much more experience under her belt, Spektor sang the song for a Haitian relief benefit, delivering it with much more confidence and force. The contrast between these readings is telling: Though technically a "better" performance, the 2010 version is ultimately not as compelling as the 2005 rendition.

"It's an ever-changing and transporting song," she said. "You go somewhere every time you hear 'Hallelujah.' You never stay put. That song is the pillar of everything."

The best-known singer to take on "Hallelujah" during the first half of the 2000s, though, was yet another Canadian, k. d. lang. In 2004, the year she released *Hymns of the 49th Parallel,* lang was one of the most respected vocalists in the world. She had won four Grammy Awards since her 1987 U.S. debut, *Angel with a Lariat.* In 1999, she was ranked number thirty-three on VH1's "100 Greatest Women in Rock & Roll," and three years later, she came in at number twenty-six on CMT's "40 Greatest Women in Country Music"—making her one of only eight women to appear on both lists.

The *Hymns* album was made up of covers of songs by Canadian writers Joni Mitchell, Neil Young, Jane Siberry, Bruce Cockburn, Ron Sexsmith, and Leonard Cohen (plus one original). The Cohen selections were "Bird on the Wire" and "Hallelujah."

"The concept of the album was the spiritual nature of

the Canadian songwriter," said lang. "I wanted to make a modern, conceptual hymn record. I think with all of these writers, there's a heavy spiritual thread, and an equanimity and a compassion running through the lyrics in a way that's totally available to the listener, without any sort of guidance of the moral of the story; it's always up to you. And I think that in general Canadians are pretty open in terms of that.

"I don't know why Canadians are that way. I don't know if it's being sandwiched between the European and the American cultures, I don't know if it's because we have to live through winter every year, or because we have such a huge amount of space to live with. We have a totally different relationship to the environment. That's what the *Hymns* record was about."

Growing up in the province of Alberta, lang heard Cohen's records and was familiar with his "Hallelujah," though she said that Buckley's recording "defined the song in popular culture." She believes that the lyrics grew out of Cohen's sense of "the irony of being a human being and looking for the religion in sex"—a concise summary of the dichotomy at the heart of the song, and central to much of Cohen's work.

In lang's analysis, Buckley picked up on and emphasized the aspect of the song focused on desire, but she thinks that its ongoing resonance actually comes from its spiritual essence.

"Leonard is a Buddhist, I'm a Buddhist," she said. "I know he wasn't Buddhist when he wrote it, but he has that sensibility. I think spirituality in general in our society has been diffused into some sort of relationship between the pop culture and our own personal pillars that we create for ourselves. As culture moved forward, we were counting on God less, and people settled into some sort of spirituality that they created themselves, and a lot of it has to do with incorporating their own human desire. We're greatly craving some sort of spirituality in music.

"It's a song for meditating, for pondering bigger issues, moral issues. I think that's why it has such an impact on today's society—because we're mulling over a lot, we're not being rammed with somebody else's doctrine down our throat, we're coming up with our own. It's less structured, less guided, and more individual, more personal."

When she first chose "Hallelujah" for inclusion on *Hymns of the 49th Parallel,* however, lang wasn't thinking as much about the song's cultural or spiritual significance as she was about its musicality—maybe because, at the time, it hadn't yet fully ascended to universal status. She's quick to point out that the aesthetic element is as crucial as the content to the song's legacy.

" 'Hallelujah' has a lot to gravitate toward as a singer," she said. "The structure of the song, the melody of the refrain; it gives you a lot to work with. I think when I first recorded it, I was more into the melodic structure, the flow of the song, and then as I performed it live and lived the cinematic, narrative nature of the song, it became infinitely interesting to me. I never get tired of living the experience of the emotional scenario—the ironic resolve in getting to the chorus and acquiescing to the fact that the very nature of being human is desire itself.

"It's up to interpretation. It just boils down to that. It's applicable to whatever you need it to be applicable to."

The version of "Hallelujah" that lang recorded is leisurely, expansive. It retains the contemplative nature of the lyric, but the sheer force and clarity of her voice give it a triumphal power. It's much closer to a public shout to the heavens than Buckley's solitary incantation, and if lang's delivery lacks the humor and irony of Cohen's, she adds a melodic pull and sense of purpose. Where Jeff Buckley's is the "Hallelujah" of a sullen, lustful adolescent, and Leonard Cohen's conjures the hard-fought wisdom of a surviving elder, k. d. lang's "Hallelujah" is that of a thoughtful, searching, mature adult.

Cohen has often praised lang's rendition of the song over the years. His companion/collaborator Anjani Thomas said that after hearing lang perform "Hallelujah" at the Canadian Songwriters Hall of Fame in 2006, "we looked at each other and said, 'Well, I think we can lay that song to rest now! It's really been done to its ultimate, blissful state of perfection.' "

As both the soundtrack usages and the covers of "Hallelujah" were becoming pervasive, one thing becoming evident was that the song had a peculiar advantage over and above its compositional merits. Since its best-known version was already a cover, and the song's author had himself altered the lyrics almost immediately after recording it, it was somehow understood that the words were never truly considered fixed or set in stone. With Cohen's tacit approval, and Buckley not around to object, verses could be cut, lyrics could be changed, with no real sense of betraying the song's meaning.

For a song as weird as "Hallelujah," this open invitation to experiment and adjust is perhaps its greatest allure. Depending on preference and context, the different elements—religion, sex, hope, despair, love, death—can be turned up or down at will. Certainly, the "I remember when I moved in you" verse was often abandoned, especially for religious or charitable uses. Sometimes even "She tied you to a kitchen chair" was a little too much for the setting. But with its abstract and disconnected imagery, the song's contradictions and nuances could easily be elided, which gave "Hallelujah" a versatility that went beyond its ambiguities.

"I tend to be a wordy person, and I think every verse is so beautiful that I just couldn't part with one of them," said Kate Voegele. "But I think the song has this unbelievable ability to take a personal concept and elevate it to the universal. So I think people pick and choose the verses because they're all sort of little stories within themselves, and no matter what order you sing them in or hear them in, it means something."

"It's very open to interpretation," said Lee DeWyze, the 2010 *American Idol* champion. DeWyze sang one highly abbreviated edit of the song on the show, when the stakes were high and the contest had come down to three finalists, but he has altered the choice of lyrics on his own subsequent tours. "The only other song like it would be the national anthem. Because there's no one national anthem that everyone's like, 'That's the one.' People just do it however they want. 'Hallelujah' is one of those songs that doesn't feel like it has an owner. When people sing it now, it's almost like, 'This is my song.' "

Some artists offer more practical reasons for the revisions of the lyric. "I'll drop the fourth verse if I'm running out of time," said Brandi Carlile. "A lot of times, I close with it, so if I'm playing a union hall and I have six minutes before it goes into overtime pay, I've got to drop a verse." This ability to truncate would prove invaluable as the song became a staple of televised singing competitions.

The impressionistic composition of the verses, with shifting perspective and nonlinear narrative, means that there's no functional loss or disruption in meaning if verses are skipped or moved. "I think with that song," said Rufus Wainwright, "as is the case with a lot of Leonard's work, there are certain phrases that really jump out and hit you in different ways, and mean different things to different people—'learn to shoot at someone who outdrew you.' I think it's more about those tiny nuggets of words than any broad meaning, but then once 'hallelujah,' that word, is placed in there, it kind of gathers up all of these elements, which is the essence of existence anyway: There's no general theme for the world—it's all little tiny pieces."

Consider the contrast with one of the few songs that goes on a list with "Hallelujah" as a modern-day anthem— John Lennon's "Imagine." Yoko Ono has said that she constantly has to turn down requests for people who want to record the song and change just one word. The possible uses for "Imagine" multiply dramatically if she would allow singers to modify the line "Nothing to kill or die for / And no religion, too"—which she refuses to let them do, feeling that a change to the less radical "And one religion, too" would interfere with the song's message and intentions too much.

CeeLo Green performed "Imagine" on NBC's 2012 New Year's Eve broadcast from Times Square, changing the lyric to "And all religion's true." Predictably, Lennon loyalists, especially in the online world, immediately went nuts: Rolling Stone reported a typical tweet, from @geekysteven, which read, "The whole point of that lyric is that religion causes harm. If 'all religion's true' it would be a pretty bleak place."

In the end, though, Lennon's recording of "Imagine" is so iconic it can never truly be challenged, or even fully re-imagined, by a cover; as with "Bridge over Troubled Water," with Art Garfunkel's distinct vocal, any new performance is instantly, however subconsciously, assessed in relation to the original. And, as CeeLo learned, any alteration of the lyric dramatically changes the song's message in ways that many listeners are unwilling to accept.

"Hallelujah," on the other hand, isn't fixed and formalized in the same way. Before it had even penetrated the general population's consciousness, it had demonstrated that it is capable of withstanding multiple modifications, possibly resulting in a change of its emphasis, but not its essence. This fluidity helped open countless doors for the song over the years.

In October 2004, Leonard Cohen released a new album, titled *Dear Heather*. It had been only three years since his last album—the shortest time between new music from him since the 1970s. Though the record contains some affecting moments, it has a bit of a patchwork feel and in the end is one of Cohen's least satisfying albums. Nonetheless, *Dear Heather* reached Number 131 on the *Billboard* charts—Cohen's highest ranking since *Songs from a Room* in 1969.

Newfound appreciation for Cohen was also apparent in a series of tribute concerts assembled by the producer Hal Willner, titled "Came So Far for Beauty." The 2005 Australian production of the show—which included such unassailably über-hip artists as Nick Cave, Beth Orton, Jarvis Cocker, and more—would later become the foundation for a documentary by Lian Lunson called *I'm Your Man*. The film also included such star turns as U2 backing Cohen on a performance of "Tower of Song," filmed in a tiny New York nightclub.

In the film, Rufus Wainwright reprised his version of "Hallelujah," as he did at most of the "Came So Far for Beauty" shows, accompanied by his sister Martha. The "Hallelujah" performance Willner now seems proudest of, however, came at the 2006 show in Dublin, when Wainwright couldn't make the trip.

"We thought, 'Oh, man, what are we going to do with this now? Wait a minute, let's break this down, let's look at it differently,' " he said. "I'd heard a number of versions, and I thought it was time to give it a different look." For this show, he matched Irish post-punk singer-songwriter Gavin Friday with eccentric Canadian vocalist Mary Margaret O'Hara for a cacophonous, irreverent "Hallelujah" that polarized the audience.

"It was this outrageous, two-sided thing," said Willner, who has always championed a slightly cockeyed approach to his tribute projects, preferring provocation over canonization. "We weren't being funny, we were just incorporating something else, and the reactions were unbelievable. I think Leonard would have loved it, but I always said that if the artist hears what we're doing and likes it, we didn't do our job."

Meantime, the cult and the myth of Jeff Buckley were continuing to grow. In 2004, Buckley's "Hallelujah" was included as number 259 in *Rolling Stone's* list of the 500 Greatest Songs of All Time. In 2006, the Q magazine readers' poll that had previously placed *Grace* at number seventy-five on the list of Greatest Albums of All Time was taken again—and this time *Grace* ranked thirteenth. The same year, *Mojo* magazine named *Grace* its #1 "Modern Classic."

This ongoing discovery and reevaluation of Buckley's music was being matched by a steady stream of new product. The *Grace* material was repackaged and extended with the release of the *Grace EPs* box set and then of a two-disc "Legacy Edition" of the album. In 2000, the *Mystery White Boy* album collected live performances from 1995 and '96 by Buckley with his band, recorded around the world. "Hallelujah," played in Seattle as a medley with the Smiths' "I Know It's Over," closed the album.

Perhaps most important, the Legacy Edition of *Live at Sin-é* was released in 2003, expanding the original EP's four songs to two full CDs, and giving a true sense of the now-legendary, freewheeling Monday night sessions on St. Mark's Place. This package also concluded with "Hallelujah"—a riveting, nine-plus-minute solo excursion, full of wailing incantation and guitar wizardry that certainly confirms the grasp Buckley had of the song before he took it into the recording studio.

For better or worse, following the song's initial burst into the public imagination, the years from 2001 to 2005 solidified the standing of "Hallelujah" in numerous ways, and broadened its reach. Having fanned out across the globe, and conquered the small and large screens, the song was increasingly becoming part of pop's common vocabulary, and the momentum it was gaining showed no signs of slowing down.

CHAPTER NINE

While the "Hallelujah" industry was expanding, it turned out that Leonard Cohen himself was not fully able to reap the benefits. In 2004, he discovered that for years, his manager, Kelley Lynch, had been defrauding him of millions of dollars, siphoning off a large amount of money that he presumed was being amassed for his retirement. The situation turned into a legal nightmare when Lynch simply disappeared. Cohen, now seventy, sued Lynch, accusing her of stealing $5 million from his personal accounts and investments while he lived at Mt. Baldy.

"It was a long, ongoing problem of a disastrous and relentless indifference to my financial situation," he told the *New York Times*. "I didn't even know where the bank was."

In March 2006, a judge granted Cohen a default judgment in the case, ordering Lynch to pay $9.5 million. She ignored the suit and did not respond to a subpoena issued for her financial records. It was generally assumed that Cohen would never be able to collect the awarded amount, nor any of the money with which Lynch absconded. He suddenly found himself needing to make decisions about his career based on economics, which didn't seem to sit well with the usual pace of his output.

As much of a disaster as Cohen's financial situation was, it turned out that things with Lynch actually got much uglier than anyone suspected. Years later, it emerged that after he dismissed her as his manager, she began calling and e-mailing him with hostile, sometimes threatening messages. Cohen obtained numerous restraining orders against her in California and in Colorado, where she had moved. Lynch's actions continued to escalate until, in 2012, Cohen pressed charges against her—five counts of violating protective orders and two counts of repeatedly contacting Cohen with the intent to annoy or harass.

When the trial opened in April, Cohen was the first witness to appear in Los Angeles County Superior Court. He testified that he and Lynch had a business and personal relationship for about seventeen years; she had been an assistant to his former manager, Marty Machat, and took over in the role when Machat died, in 1988. He said that at one point, they had a "brief" intimate relationship.

Cohen said that as soon as he fired Lynch as his manager, the threatening messages began, with some voice mails lasting up to ten minutes and e-mails that ran as long as fifty pages. "It started with just a few now and then, but it eventually accelerated to twenty or thirty a day," he said. The caller leveled accusations and threats at him and said that he "needed to be taken down and shot."

"It makes me feel very conscious about my surroundings," Cohen said. "Every time I see a car slow down, I get worried." He added, "My sense of alarm has increased over the years as the volume of e-mails has increased." (The case focused specifically on messages left between February 2011 and January 2012.)

Over several days, prosecutors played voice mails said to be from Lynch, peppered with obscenities, sexual references, and accusations that Cohen was abusing drugs. Many of the calls were said to have been made when Lynch was intoxicated. Prosecutors also displayed ten binders filled with printed e-mails sent to Cohen, his attorneys, and others.

According to the *Los Angeles Times,* Lynch, who pleaded not guilty, "occasionally smiled as voice mails from 2011 were played for jurors." In his opening statements, Michael Kelly, a public defender representing Lynch, said the case was "very much about relationships and how relationships oftentimes get messy." He said Cohen's attorneys had "done everything in their power" to undermine his client's credibility.

As time went on, it seems that Lynch grew bolder in her

actions, in recent years writing lengthy screeds not only to Cohen, but also to various bloggers, journalists, and government officials. A series of Facebook messages signed by Kelley Lynch and sent to writer Mikal Gilmore, who has profiled Cohen several times (once for a story I assigned at *Spin* magazine in 2001), were posted under the name "Cyber Terrorism" to a site called River Deep, which is devoted mostly to the elaborate and passionate defense of producer Phil Spector against his murder charge and all other alleged misdeeds—and if these are representative of the messages Cohen was receiving, they are creepy stuff indeed.

The writer repeatedly and obsessively attempts to refute Cohen's story that Spector had a gun in the studio during the *Death of a Ladies' Man* sessions. In a message posted May 28, 2011, the writer calls Cohen "a great liar; fraud; and con artist" and later says he is "an out of control lunatic and his history of mental illness, drug and alcohol abuse, etc. does not help." She claims that he made the accusation against Spector because "Cohen committed serious criminal tax fraud (with penalties & interest in the amount of $30 million) and thought perhaps the District Attorney could help him and visa versa [sic]."

Another message, posted that same day, says that "Phil Spector thinks Cohen is a closet Partridge Family groupie and he and I both believe Cohen is a porn artist with biblical references." The writer says that "we were never lovers although he repeatedly attempted to have sex with me when I would visit him on Mt. Baldy," and implies that Cohen "molested" his own daughter. A message posted the following day, May 29, finds the writer claiming that "this man has stolen from me; destroyed my life; permitted me to end up homeless; had his lawyer file a declaration in my son's custody matter . . . and recently had his unconscionable thug lawyers threaten to have me arrested when I requested information I require for a complete forensic accounting in order to amend my federal tax returns and determine the amount of the theft."

Presented with numerous communications like this, the jury reached a guilty verdict against Lynch within hours of receiving the case. A week later, she was sentenced to eighteen months in jail (though she will likely spend much less time behind bars because of prison overcrowding in California), plus five years' probation, and was ordered to attend anger-management sessions, psychological training, and alcohol education sessions.

Prior to the sentencing, Lynch blamed prosecutors for carrying out a "vicious attack" on her, though she added, "I do believe that I have engaged in excessive and unauthorized rambling."

"It gives me no pleasure . . . to see my onetime friend shackled to a chair in a court of law," said Cohen, "her considerable gifts bent to the service of darkness, deceit, and revenge."

With this harassment as a backdrop, and faced with the reality of having only a few hundred thousand dollars saved, in 2005, the seventy-one-year-old Cohen had little choice but to get back to work; he had already begun to sell off his assets and had taken out a mortgage on his house. In May of 2006, he released a collection of poetry and drawings titled *Book of Longing*, which topped the best-seller lists in Canada. That same month, his backup singer and current girlfriend, Anjani Thomas—whom he first met when she participated in the *Various Positions* sessions in 1984—put out the album *Blue Alert*, which was made up entirely of songs cowritten by Cohen, many of them constructed from writings they found in his notebooks that he had never completed.

"Finances were a huge factor," Thomas said. "It was like, 'We've got to make a record, make some money.' It was a terribly pressurized situation, full of shock and awe and disbelief—so in the midst of that, running to the studio and banging on a piano was the fun part."

The album, a pleasant, almost smooth-jazz take on Leonard Cohen, was well reviewed. The release of the album and the book also roughly coincided with the general release of the *I'm Your Man* documentary. Cohen even made a couple of rare appearances on stage, performing a few songs with Anjani in New York and Paris. It proved to be a fine confluence of activities for an artist who needed a quick infusion of both income and visibility.

"I'm happy that all these events came to completion around the same time," Cohen told me in 2006 for a *New York Times* story. "It's useful in a certain way—since I'm not in the marketplace that often, it creates a certain possible invitation to listen."

As he did a slate of promotion for these various projects, journalists were finally starting to ask Cohen about the resurgence of "Hallelujah." In a March 2006 interview for *CBS Sunday Morning* (which was filmed but never aired), he addressed the ongoing interest in the song.

"It's wonderful," he said. "The path of that song has been so curious to me, because when I first put that song out, perhaps my own version of it was not distinguished—it certainly doesn't compare to the subsequent versions of it. But when I put the record out, no one remarked on the song. And then, years later, it started to appear."

He mentioned that Cale's version had been used in *Shrek*, and continued, "Then suddenly many, many people were using it. It seems to have discovered its place. I was very, very surprised at how it was resurrected, because it really was lost."

Cohen recognized that there was an interest in "Hallelujah." What he may not yet have fully realized, though, was the extent to which the song would prove the key to offering the larger world an "invitation to listen" to his work.

• • •

By this time, "Hallelujah" was no longer just a song that young artists could present as a new discovery and deploy as a way to prove how deep they were or increase their credibility. In 2007, a poll of fifty songwriters conducted by Q magazine listed Buckley's "Hallelujah" among the all-time Top Ten Greatest Tracks. In the entry for the song, R&B singer John Legend called it "as near perfect as you can get . . . one of the most beautiful pieces of recorded music I've ever heard."

Now it was firmly carved into the Mt. Rushmore of contemporary song—a challenge for established rock stars to tackle, and demonstrate that they, too, were hip enough to draw from the power of this composition. In the next few years, veteran artists such as Willie Nelson and former Doobie Brother Michael McDonald would record "Hallelujah."

These performances both proved surprising. At this point, you might expect that such old hands would give the song a stately, sober reading, using the melody to showcase their distinctive, weathered voices. But both singers gave "Hallelujah" unexpected spins, and both clearly approached it as a Leonard Cohen song rather than as a Jeff Buckley song.

Nelson recorded it on his *Songbird* album, an inspired if ultimately disappointing experiment that matched him with young gun country rocker Ryan Adams. Adams picked the material, which included songs by Fleetwood Mac and Gram Parsons, as well as some Nelson classics and "Amazing Grace."

In the arrangement Adams did for "Hallelujah," Nelson sings the verses from *Various Positions*, with a pedal steel guitar and a harmonica adding a bluesy feel. Rather than explode into the chorus, Nelson sings the payoff word almost perfunctorily, tossing it off twice rather than the usual four times—there's nothing celebratory here; he presents it as something of an afterthought. Only toward the end, when a choir somewhat incongruously takes over the chorus, does Shotgun Willie's "Hallelujah" surrender to the song's most obvious sentiments.

As for McDonald, he took the song in an even more surprising direction. On the *Soul Speak* album—which encompassed covers ranging from Van Morrison to Bob Marley—he sings the lyrics from the *Cohen Live* arrangement, opening with the "Baby, I've been here before" verse rather than the now-iconic "secret chord" verse. He performs a soul-jazz version of the song, and bravely takes liberties with the melody, opening up the standard singsong simplicity and moving away from the waltz feel underpinning almost every other rendition.

McDonald's throaty, oft-parodied baritone, as always, is a matter of taste, but he definitely gets points for ambition. Like Nelson's, his "Hallelujah" is the song of a survivor, not a young romantic.

McDonald had been asked to participate in a Cohen tribute at UCLA by his friend, longtime Cohen backup singer Perla Batalla. Other performers on the bill included Jackson Browne, Don Was, and rediscovered soul titan Howard Tate. Batalla sent McDonald some material to choose from, and he was drawn to "Hallelujah," a song he didn't previously know.

"I came up with this idea for a classic R&B 6/8 feel, changed the key, and voiced the chords a little differently," he said. He also let the introduction go longer, pulling the melody up front for a while before getting to the words. "I strove to loosen it up a bit and let the lyrics fall in a wider space—on the records, the words come in really soon."

The show came in the middle of the sessions for his *Soul Speak* album, and when he returned to the studio the morning after the performance, he decided that he should record the song. "It's one of the most beautiful, honest lyrics ever written about love," he said. "It stands apart in its honesty, in addressing the part of love that's lonesome, desperate. Love isn't just a pink cloud that you ride around on—love is what it is, and hallelujah for that. Don't have grand notions or huge expectations because then you miss what love really is, you miss the real gift of it."

The recording that Batalla had initially sent him was indeed the "Hallelujah" from *Cohen Live,* and McDonald said that even after he listened to the studio versions, he chose to stick with the less-conventional edit of the lyrics. "I just preferred the verses I heard on the live album," he said. "The way the conversation started was so much more personal and honest, it really set up the whole idea of the song."

As for the familiar opening lines, he claims that he just doesn't miss them. "Not that I didn't like that verse," he said. "I thought it was clever wordplay, but it didn't hold the same emotional feel for me."

McDonald has kept "Hallelujah" in his live set ever since, and stripped it down more and more as time goes on. "It's a song you can't take down to the bare essence enough," he said. On his most recent tour, he and co-headliner Boz Scaggs performed it as the show's encore, accompanied by just piano and guitar. "No matter how many times I do the song, it goes deeper every time," he said. "It's like a good book—three hundred times later, you feel like you're just getting it for the first time. You could never really exhaust the feeling of that song.

"I love that it took this iconic, religious word and returned it to its actual meaning—that love is above and beyond all other things, it transcends all things on the planet. No matter how beat up I am by the world around me, as long as I recognize love and give it its due, hallelujah."

Moving further up the celebrity chain, Bon Jovi performed the song on an *Unplugged* session and for a live DVD—though Jon Bon Jovi confesses that when he first heard "Hallelujah," he was among the many people who thought that Jeff Buckley had written it.

"I saw Buckley at a club called the Saint in Asbury Park that couldn't have held more than a hundred people," he said. "I heard him sing 'Hallelujah' and I said, 'That's the hit!' And somebody said, 'Nice going, genius—that's a Leonard Cohen song.' And I said, 'Well, it's the only song [Buckley's] got.'"

Bon Jovi may not have known who wrote "Hallelujah," but he said that he instantly keyed in to the intention of the lyrics, which he believes many interpreters miss. "I got the meaning of 'Hallelujah' right away," he said. "I got the irony, got the sexuality. I won't name the artists who have no clue of what's inside those words, but I've often said that people in America know the chorus to that song, people in the rest of the world know the verses."

Bon Jovi started performing the song in smaller settings and at private events. Initially, it seemed listeners didn't know the song and assumed it was an original, but by the time he had it in rotation for the 2007 Lost Highway tour, his audience knew the song not only from his band's own version, but also from all the other covers.

As for the song's popularity, he said, "I can only guess, but maybe it's the simplicity of the chorus—sometimes simplicity gets people's attention. How many Dylan songs are there that we're amazed by, but they don't do that?" But, he's quick to add, that directness is contrasted with the complexity of the verses, including the explication of the chord sequence in the opening lines. "If you were really trying to write simple, you wouldn't engage the audience in music theory in the first verse," he said. "It shows that he's an instinctual writer; he's just saying it.

"When you get to that last verse, I can't even explain it to somebody who hasn't stood in my spot and looked out—you zero in and deliver that to somebody, and you will see an electrical charge. . . . I'm being polite with the language."

Bon Jovi guitarist Richie Sambora added that for him, the message of "Hallelujah" doesn't feel far from the intentions of the band's own songs. "Look at 'Livin' on a Prayer,' " he said. "Our songs are all optimistic, in a world that has a lot of problems, so a song like 'Hallelujah' fits into what we're doing. It's kind of a perfect song, to bring spirituality into everyday life and relationships like that.

"Just to tackle that word *hallelujah* is daunting, and to bring so much culture and sociology into a song is pretty strange. But there's a spirituality in Leonard Cohen that he found in relationships, human being to human being, and as songwriters, that's something we're all trying to conjure."

Much to the dismay of many Leonard Cohen and Jeff Buckley fans—who routinely rate Bon Jovi's "Hallelujah" as the worst version of the song, or use it as an example of its most inappropriate interpretations—Cohen himself has expressed his admiration for the band's take; when *Rolling*

Stone asked him for his favorite "Hallelujah" covers, he mentioned k. d. lang and Bon Jovi.

Jon Bon Jovi's vocal is certainly more melodramatic than most, closer to a brawny power ballad and not as "cold and broken," but after listening to a lot of weepy and fragile deliveries of the lyric, there's something bracing about hearing it sung with some muscle. He feels no obligation to step delicately through these words; he hits them hard and sells them like a real rock song. It may not be an especially profound reading, but it certainly shows that the song can hold up to a stadium crowd and still pack an emotional punch.

Members of Cohen's generation, or maybe, like Jon Bon Jovi, the next age group down, weren't the only ones taking "Hallelujah" to bigger audiences. Popular young rock bands Fall Out Boy and Paramore found a different way to pay homage to the song, working references to "Hallelujah" into their own originals.

Paramore, fronted by charismatic redhead Hayley Williams, was nominated for the Best New Artist Grammy Award in 2007, losing to Amy Winehouse. On their platinum-selling 2007 album *Riot!*, the band recorded a straight-ahead upbeat love song of their own called "Hallelujah" ("This time we're not giving up / Let's make it last forever"). When they played the song live, though, they worked a section of the Cohen song into the performance, as documented on the gold-certified live album and DVD *The Final Riot!*

The performance opens with the guitarist playing the familiar, Buckley-esque intro figure, followed by Williams delivering a full-throated pass at Cohen's first verse. The shrieks of the audience are audible when she begins, and the crowd takes over the chorus when it comes; it's clear that Paramore's young fans already know this song. After the chorus, the band kicks into their original—with no particular connection to the other "Hallelujah" beyond the title, but with the points already scored for connecting to something familiar yet unexpected, with the history and sentiment these young fans carried with them from *Shrek* and their favorite TV dramas.

Fall Out Boy, a pop-punk band who took their name from a fictional comic book character referred to on *The Simpsons,* make a more subtle use of "Hallelujah," but one that is apparently just as effective. Singer Patrick Stump recalls that it was an odd set of circumstances that landed a piece of Cohen's composition into their song.

Stump writes all of Fall Out Boy's music, while bass player Pete Wentz writes the lyrics. Their usual method is that Wentz hands over notebooks full of poems, lines, and ideas, and Stump pulls out the words or sections that inspire ideas for melodies.

"I was going through his stuff," said Stump, "and I saw a line about 'Hum Hallelujah.' Pete had a more religious upbringing than me, so I think he meant a literal church hallelujah, but I liked it being ambiguous, and it kept evoking the 'Hallelujah' melody. We were working on the bridge and couldn't think what we were doing, and I sang the [Cohen] melody, really kind of as a joke, over the instrumental. I really had no intention of using it, but Pete came in right then and he said, 'That was awesome! What is that?' So I had to explain it to him.

"But the funny thing was, he was like, 'I know that, it's an old church song.' And I had to tell him that no, it isn't. He knew that it was familiar, it was just something in music history at this point—and this is before *American Idol* and all that."

Stump routinely used the Buckley version of the song when he was singing for himself or warming up his voice; he claims that he probably sang it "a thousand times," but had never thought to use it in the context of the band, and was wary when the idea presented itself.

"There's a real responsibility," he said. "I respect the music that I care about, and I didn't want to miscontextualize something that people hold near and dear, or butcher somebody else's masterwork. When we decided to use that melody, I thought, 'Well, now this has to be a good song.' That section kept a sheen of beauty—borrowed beauty—over the whole thing. It added reverence to what would have been a cheeky pop-punk song."

Fall Out Boy's audience reacted immediately to the inclusion of the chorus of "Hallelujah" as the bridge in "Hum Hallelujah." Though the song wasn't released as a single, it consistently received one of the biggest responses in the band's live set.

"No one ever told me about 'Hallelujah,'" said Stump. "I had to do a little bit of investigative work to get to it myself, to find Buckley's album, and then Leonard Cohen's. So one of the biggest surprises was when our audience flipped out at that song every night.

"People keep finding the song in new ways. It has a really enduring life. I've had kids talk to me about 'Hallelujah' as if they were the only ones who knew about it—it's a cult classic, like the world's biggest sleeper hit. It's like joining a club."

That club extended far beyond the borders of the U.S. and the UK. In some of the countries that had embraced Jeff Buckley most enthusiastically while he was alive, "Hallelujah" was now breaking away from his body of work and gaining even more momentum. In 2006, an all-star Norwegian quartet of Espen Lind (a former Artist of the Year winner at the Norwegian Grammys, and cowriter of such hits as Beyoncé's "Irreplaceable" and Train's "Hey Soul Sister"), Kurt Nilsen (winner of the *World Idol* competition), Chilean-born Alejandro Fuentes, and Askil Holm released a cover of the song, which became the fastest-selling hit in Norway's history.

Their "Hallelujah" reached Number One on the country's singles chart, going ten times platinum in two weeks and eventually selling more than 250,000 copies (twenty-five times platinum). The song stayed in the Norwegian Top 20 for thirty-seven weeks, and gave its title to the foursome's *Hallelujah Live* album, which also went to Number One. Incredibly, the video for their pleasant, only occasionally overwrought "Hallelujah" has been watched on YouTube almost exactly the same number of times as all of the Jeff Buckley clips combined—a staggering fifty million views.

As the tenth anniversary of Buckley's death approached, his following seemed to keep growing every year, and to become more formalized. In 2007, there were tribute events held around the world—in Australia, Iceland, France, Macedonia, and many more countries. (Currently, there are two ongoing, annual Jeff Buckley tribute events: Chicago's two-day event at Uncommon Ground and a yearly New York City tribute called "An Evening with Jeff Buckley.")

Incredibly, Buckley's own thirteen-year-old recording

of "Hallelujah," which had never been released as a single, began to show up on European pop charts itself. In 2006, on the heels of the Lind/Nilsen/Fuentes/Holm hit, it went to Number Seven in Norway, meaning that the song reached the Top Ten in two different versions in one year. The next year, it hit Number Five in Sweden.

During the week of March 15, 2008, "Hallelujah" was the single most downloaded song in France. Eleven years after his death, Jeff Buckley had his first Number One hit.

CHAPTER TEN

For the next phase of "Hallelujah"-mania, once again, Northern Europe got there early. In 2007, Amanda Jenssen sang "Hallelujah" in the semifinals of the Swedish edition of *Idol.* She eventually lost the championship vote by a few percentage points, but her version of the song became an online hit, and when her debut album was released, it went to Number One.

This performance was a harbinger of things to come. The year 2008 would prove to be yet another landmark in the journey of "Hallelujah," this time through a different kind of usage on television. It was the year in which the singing competitions discovered the song and, yet again, propelled it to new levels of visibility and popularity.

In the U.S., Jason Castro performed the song during the round of sixteen on *American Idol,* which was devoted to songs from the 1980s. (Its inclusion may have been a surprise to any of the viewers who knew it only through Buckley's 1994 recording.) The dreadlocked Colombian-American singer gave a simple performance, almost shockingly clean amid the overwrought melismas of most *Idol* singers. He gave an especially nice vocal wink on the "you don't really care for music, do ya?" line. Though Castro played guitar, and even ukulele, on other episodes of the show, this time he sang with no instrument in his hands.

It's kind of alarming to go back and watch single-song clips from *Idol* in isolation, and realize just how brief these performances are. Castro sings for barely ninety seconds, enough to get through the song's first verse and the "marble arch" verse. It's quite a tribute to the resilience of this lyric—this edit removes virtually all of the spirituality and every bit of the sexuality of Cohen's words, leaving just a vague sense of romantic yearning. In Castro's "Hallelujah," the central line becomes "love is not a victory march," which is a strong idea but not the song's usual focal point.

Still, he used his time well and, whatever the limitations, he made an impression; judge Randy Jackson registered his fondness for the Cohen and Buckley recordings, and said that following them was "a tall order, because they really did it, they worked it out." *Idol* majordomo Simon Cowell, who would become a key figure in the progress of "Hallelujah," called Castro's performance "absolutely brilliant."

It left its mark with the public as well. Later, MTV.com

proclaimed Castro's "Hallelujah" to be "one of the best *Idol* performances of all time." Castro would eventually finish fourth in that year's contest, and he included a recording of "Hallelujah" on his 2010 debut album, which reached the Top 20.

More surprising, though, was that immediately following Castro's performance, Buckley's recording of the song skyrocketed on iTunes. His "Hallelujah" sold 178,000 digital downloads in the week following Castro's performance—the highest boost in sales a song had ever received from an *Idol* cover—to debut at Number One on *Billboard*'s "Hot Digital Songs" chart. It was the first time Buckley's version of the song reached any *Billboard* chart, as well as his first-ever U.S. Number One. Within a matter of weeks, the single was certified gold, and then platinum.

Later in the year, Simon Cowell would make good on the fact that he had called "Hallelujah" (specifying the Buckley recording) "one of [his] favorite songs of all time" when a twenty-year-old R&B singer named Alexandra Burke reached the finals of the 2008 edition of *The X Factor* in England. After Cowell and the show's producers told her that the song she would be singing in the final would be "Hallelujah," Burke said that, initially, she was "gutted."

"I thought, 'Cor, I've lost already, I'm never gonna do a justifiable version of that song,'" said Burke a few years later, on the phone from London. "My mum has been in the business for a long time, and when I was told that was the song chosen, I called her and said, 'I'm not going to win, that song is never going to suit me.' But my mum said, 'Calm down, listen to the song, and call me back.'

"I grew up listening to Motown and soul records, and I realized that there were all these different versions of 'Hallelujah,' but there wasn't a soulful one, and maybe that was my way to put my own spin on it. I called my mum back and told her that I was going to Whitney-fy it, really make it soulful, and she burst into tears on the phone."

Still, Burke had questions. She heard the different verses used in the different recordings, and she said that she asked the producers, "Hang on, which version are we doing?" Maybe because it was the final round, a little more time could be given over to the actual music, so she was presented with an edit that had three verses—in addition to the first and last of the Buckley version, she also sang the "She tied you to a kitchen chair" verse (which also perhaps displayed a bit more confidence in the sophistication of European, as opposed to American, viewers).

"When they picked the verses, the whole meaning came clear to me," said Burke. "I had asked my mum, 'Explain to me what the song means.' And she said, 'Yes, it's dark, but people take in their own kind of meaning, and it's also loving.' The 'maybe there's a God above' verse, that's my favorite. That boils down to my religion, which for me is really the whole meaning."

No doubt, Burke's "Hallelujah" is a powerhouse. On her *X Factor* performance and then on the subsequent studio recording, the first two verses come relatively straight, with little embellishment against a simple arrangement. But there's definitely a sense of calm before the storm. After the second chorus, there's a brief instrumental break, and then Burke explodes into the final verse—on the show, you can see the audience starting to go wild—backed by a gospel choir. It is, in fact, reminiscent of dramatic Whitney Houston ballads like "I Will Always Love You," in which Houston famously built in a brief pause before the roof-raising climax.

Burke digs into that final verse, delivering "Hallelujah" as salvation. "It's not a cry that you hear at night / it's not someone who's seen the light"—hers is a hallelujah that is open to all, a reward for faith rather than a resigned surrender. Ironically, in some ways it was a return to the spirit of celebration that was intended, but came to be so easily overlooked, in the *Various Positions* version.

Burke might not offer all of the meanings that Cohen wrote into these words, but she sings with a clear sense of purpose and a passionate drive. Her take may flatten out the poetry, but it's damn near irresistible.

The reaction from the public was staggering. More than

eight million votes were cast by UK viewers, and Burke was crowned *X Factor* champion. "Hallelujah" was instantly released as the "winner's single." The song, offering a spirit of joy and uplift in time for the holiday season, became the all-time European record holder for single sales over a period of twenty-four hours, selling 105,000 copies in one day on its way to becoming the top-selling song of the year in the UK. By January 2009, sales of Burke's "Hallelujah" had passed one million copies, which made her the first British female solo artist to reach that milestone.

There is an odd tradition in the UK of making a very big deal out of which song is the country's Number One hit on Christmas Day. In recent years, there have been campaigns to whip up support for old Rage Against the Machine songs and even John Cage's silent 4'33" in a bid for them to come in as the Christmas Number One.

When Jeff Buckley fans, upset by the commercial delivery and slick production of Burke's "Hallelujah," saw the instant popularity and rocket-fueled sales of the record, they responded with a campaign to promote Buckley's version on the Christmas charts. In the end, Buckley's single rose all the way to Number Two—though almost a half a million copies behind Burke—while, for good measure, Leonard Cohen's 1984 original came in at Number 36.

It marked the first time in more than forty years that the same composition held the top two spots on the singles chart. Martin Talbot, managing director of the Official Charts Company, noted that the positions were "remarkable for a twenty-five-year-old song which has never previously reached the Top 40."

The fact that the popularity of "Hallelujah" was reaching new heights in the aftermath of exposure on a televised singing contest may have been improbable, but at least it was understandable. (It was also sung on *Canadian Idol* and recorded, in another hit version, by the Dutch *X Factor* champion.) More incredible, though, was the way in which this resurgence continued after these phenomena had died down, and the ripples continued to be felt around the world.

In such countries as Sweden, Austria, and Switzerland, Jeff Buckley's "Hallelujah" reached the singles charts separate times in 2008, 2009, and 2010. In 2009, the Buckley track was ranked number three on the Australian radio station Triple J's "Hottest 1001 of All Time," a listener poll held every decade.

On yet another end of the musical spectrum, Simon Cowell found a different outlet for the song with his multinational "operatic pop" group Il Divo. In late 2008, the quartet—composed of singers from France, Spain, Switzerland, and the U.S.—included "Hallelujah" on its fourth album, *The Promise*. Where the song provided a showstopping moment for most of the singer-songwriters, solo vocalists, and rock bands who performed it, for this bravura set of voices, it marked a new level of subtlety.

According to Il Divo's David Miller, his fellow group member Sebastien Izambard had been advocating for "Hallelujah" for a while, but it took the song's success on *Idol* and *X Factor* to convince mentor Cowell to let them try it. Tellingly, Miller noted that it was one of the rare songs that all four of the singers were already familiar with: "We come from radically different countries, so if we all know a song, then probably everyone knows it."

They translated the lyrics into Spanish, taking some liberties with the words, and constructed an arrangement that Miller calls "delicate and intimate," in contrast to their usual grand presentations and big finishes. "When we listened back, we knew it was something special, unlike anything we'd ever done," he said—so much so that it was a challenge to find the right place for "Hallelujah" in Il Divo's live set. "It always has an impact with the audience, but it can be difficult to program it," he said. "After a huge song, it can almost be jarring for us to go so quiet, or it might be too much of a lullaby after too many quiet songs."

Regardless, it connected with Il Divo's listeners just as it had with so many others. *The Promise* went to Number One in the UK and Number Five in the U.S. "That word *hallelujah* means something to everyone," said Miller. "The release of joy in that word, everyone has experienced that at some point."

Even before Il Divo's recording, numerous vocal groups had been giving the song a more formal, traditional arrangement—and so, in addition to infiltrating the pop-punk world, the song was now a regular part of the light classical repertoire. Every set of National Tenors or opera-trained crooners seemed to perform "Hallelujah," and it had also become a staple for college a cappella groups and glee clubs.

It's rare but not unprecedented to see a song return to public awareness years after its day has passed, often owing to use on a soundtrack (think of Queen's "Bohemian Rhapsody" and its resurgence after the *Wayne's World* movie). It's quite possible, though, that no song has ever scaled those heights after such a long time, and then done it again and again, with little sense of either nostalgia or novelty, and somehow still managed to feel at once so familiar and so fresh.

At the end of 2007, Leonard Cohen was voted into the Rock and Roll Hall of Fame. This was followed, a few weeks later, by the singer's own bit of news—like an old trouper, Cohen announced in January of 2008 that he would be touring, getting back on the boards after fifteen years away. He made no secret of the fact that the tour was primarily motivated by financial reasons, an attempt to struggle back to security following the Lynch disaster.

At the Hall of Fame induction ceremony on March 10, Lou Reed introduced Cohen. He recalled the two of them meeting in the '60s at the Chelsea Hotel and at the nightclub Max's Kansas City. He compared Cohen's *Beautiful Losers* to the writings of William F. Burroughs, Allen Ginsberg, and Hubert Selby. "We're so lucky to be alive at the same time Leonard Cohen is," said the notoriously acerbic Reed.

Cohen's brief speech was followed by the young Irish singer/songwriter Damien Rice performing, inevitably, a solo and very Buckley-ish "Hallelujah." It is probable that very few people noticed that this particular set of lyrics was not one that Cohen had ever sung himself.

The next day, the first leg of the tour was announced. The trek began on May 11 at the 709-seat Playhouse in Fredericton, New Brunswick, and ran for eighty-five dates, concluding at England's twenty-thousand-capacity Manchester Arena. There was no way of knowing that demand would run so high for these shows that the tour would continue, relatively uninterrupted other than the first half of 2010, for more than two and a half years. In the end, Cohen played almost 250 dates around the world—mostly marathon, almost three-hour sets—from Australia to Israel to the Czech Republic, to rapturous reviews; one New Zealand critic said simply, "This was the best show I have ever seen."

Skipping on and off the stage; tipping his fedora in deference to the musicians when they took a solo; grinning in admiration as his backup singers, the Webb Sisters, turned a unison cartwheel mid-show, Cohen was a radiant presence in these concerts. Though it had been a few years since he said that his depression had lifted, the Prince of Bummers now truly presented a paternal, grateful demeanor. Given the functional motivation for the tour, it could have been something genuinely pathetic. Instead, as Cohen returned for encore after encore each night, it was proving to be his long-overdue victory lap.

One indication of the phenomenon that was developing around the tour came at England's Glastonbury Festival in June. The big controversy around the event this time was the fact that Jay-Z was the headliner, the first time a hip-hop artist was given that coveted slot. Noel Gallagher from Oasis expressed his disapproval, to which Jay-Z responded by opening his set with a cover of the band's "Wonderwall," ending with him smashing a guitar. But one of the most memorable performances came from Cohen on the festival's closing night.

"Veteran singer/songwriter Leonard Cohen inspired a Glastonbury 'moment' when he played his legendary song 'Hallelujah' during his Pyramid Stage slot at Glastonbury tonight," wrote NME.com. "The star started the song just as the sun was setting, and further delighted the massive crowd when he changed the lyric 'I told the truth, I didn't come here to fool ya' to 'I told the truth, I didn't come to Glastonbury to fool ya.' The crowd sang every chorus with Cohen, and gave him a massive ovation at the end."

Glastonbury's official website singled out the performance in its recap of the 2008 festival. "Leonard Cohen stole the entire weekend in dapper style, leading the crowd in an astonishing chorus of 'Hallelujah,' and performing a taut set of his greatest hits as the sun went down on the Festival's final day."

A few weeks after Glastonbury, Cohen's performance at the sold-out O2 Arena was filmed for the *Live in London* DVD and double-CD set. In the ever-shifting world of dwindling record sales, the album was Cohen's highest-charting in the U.S. since 1969, and, in a now-familiar pattern, hit the Top Ten in various European nations. *Entertainment Weekly* wrote that the set was "a reminder that Cohen is as gifted a performer as he is a songwriter."

As documented on the DVD, "Hallelujah" had settled into a standardized, fail-safe arrangement, complete with organ solo by Neil Larsen and, as noted above, the insertion of the host city into the "I didn't come to fool you" line. Cohen was now more carefully enunciating "you," rather than "ya," in every verse (a modification that Rufus Wainwright suspects he might have inspired). The line most people know (from covers starting with Cale's and Buckley's) as "it's not somebody who's seen the light" has evolved in

Cohen's performances into the more precise, more skeptical "it's not some pilgrim who claims to have seen the light."

Keeping in mind that these were Cohen's first performances of the song since the "Hallelujah" explosion, it's important that his own rendition still crescendoed with the "I'll stand before the Lord of Song / with nothing on my tongue but Hallelujah!" verse—lines that were unknown to fans who came to the song through Jeff Buckley, whose version concluded with the "all I ever learned from love / is how to shoot at someone who outdrew you" verse. Indeed, the tour program, which included excerpts from the lyrics to some of Cohen's best-known songs, contained the first verse and the two final verses of the original text. Whether this was intended to differentiate Cohen's song from Buckley's cover, or simply to emphasize his own priorities in the lyrics, the statement was significant.

A February 2009 appearance at New York's Beacon Theatre for fans and media served as the launch announcement for the next installment of the tour. It was intended to create—or amplify—buzz for the tour, and was the first time most of the NYC press witnessed the warmth of Cohen's new elder statesman persona. Whether it came from all the years of Zen study or from having a song that had taken over the public's consciousness, his mood and the impeccable caliber of his performance were stunning.

One highlight of the U.S. dates was an April performance at the Coachella Festival in Indio, California; Cohen
was an inspired booking for this annual gathering of the
hipster elite. Stacey Anderson was part of the team covering Coachella for Spin.com that year. "Only a few minutes
from the start time of Cohen's set, I was able to walk up and
almost reach the barrier," she said. "But the momentum
started when they rolled out the carpet and the brocade
chairs. It was very regal, and everyone saw that something
special—something very different from the normal, sweaty,
Ray-Bans-wearing bands—was happening. And when he
started, there was this magnetic pull toward his stage."

Cohen played "Hallelujah" toward the end of his set,
after the desert sun had gone down. "In the first few notes,
I heard gasps around me," Anderson remembered. "No one
thought he would hold it back, but just like the urgency of
the song is such a surprise each time you hear it, so was the
experience of 'I'm about to hear him sing this song.' I wasn't
prepared for it, and I knew it was coming.

"The song started very minimally, and built so quickly
to the audience overpowering him as they sang along. There
was no separation between his rendition of the song and
the audience's—they intervened immediately. I remember
seeing a look of genuine surprise come over his face, and he
took off his fedora and put it to his chest and nodded in appreciation, with tears in his eyes."

From "Hallelujah" on, she said, the audience stayed at Cohen's stage, transfixed, rather than moving along to other bands playing at the same time. "Usually at Coachella, people are waiting to hear the hit, or whatever song is in the Honda commercial that week, but no one left after that," she said. "I think everyone left that set really enraptured with him."

Amanda Palmer performed at Coachella that year, and planted herself by the stage to watch Cohen. When he started "Hallelujah," she recalls, "everyone that I could see shut up. It was a cultural agreement to have a moment of silence. Then everyone sang along with the choruses. It felt like church—it was fantastic."

Palmer said that her admiration for Cohen's accomplishment at the festival grew when she went from his stage to watch Morrissey's set. "It was like, have you ever done a sauna and got into a cold plunge? Morrissey [an outspoken vegetarian] was in a bad mood, because he was pissed about the meat carts. Leonard Cohen's set would have been profound anyway, but it gave me such an intense appreciation for what a fantastic showman he is."

On Spin's website, Cohen's performance was tagged the "Best Set" of the day. "How fitting that Leonard Cohen's performance of 'Hallelujah,' his most famous song, would still come as a glorious shock," wrote Anderson. "After all, that's what the melody does: It seeps into your heart and lies dormant—then erupts as pure emotion. . . . When the keys kicked up the first strains of 'Hallelujah,' those ascending notes led a seismic reaction—offstage, as an ecstatic audience sang every word back in hymnal, and onstage, where Cohen removed his hat and peered out into the audience with reverent, brimming tears."

Coachella was a remarkable moment for Cohen. It's one thing to thrill an audience made up of old fans, who have been waiting for over a decade to see you onstage. Even Glastonbury, though certainly a triumph, took place in a country (and in a part of the world) where Cohen has long been a much better known and admired figure. But winning over the hearts and minds of tens of thousands of young, jaded Americans—this was truly new territory.

"When he took off his hat to the audience, it struck me as such a pure moment, and I wondered what it looked like to him," said Anderson. "What must it look like for that crowd, so young and sweat-soaked, to be singing the song back to him?" Clearly, it was meaningful: When Cohen assembled a second DVD from the tour—*Songs from the Road,* which collected performances from different concerts around the world—the version of "Hallelujah" he included was the Coachella performance.

Needless to say, the song was now a climax in every show, received like holy scripture. It belonged in a category with seeing Bob Dylan sing "Like a Rolling Stone" or watching Bruce Springsteen perform "Born to Run"—it was an event that people simply wanted to witness, to say they had seen. It took on a power that had to do with the song's history first, its feeling second, and its details hardly at all. Every performance carried with it a sense of where this song had been, who had sung it, where and how every listener had first encountered it; it had reached a place where it was something to be experienced, rather than listened to. In the notes to *Songs from the Road*, producer Ed Sanders said that the song was "a rather predictable bet . . . [to] peg the nightly applause meter."

In these concerts, "Hallelujah" was triumphant and valedictory, but it was never dumbed down. It's probably impossible to be ironic when twenty thousand people are singing along with you; as Bill Flanagan noted, "It's kind of like 'Born in the U.S.A.'—you can say people misunderstood it as a patriotic anthem, but really, if you're standing up in front of a football stadium singing, 'Born in the U.S.A., born in the U.S.A.,' it *is* kind of a patriotic anthem."

But night after night, Cohen never betrayed the complexities of "Hallelujah." It's as if these performances were a culmination of all the years and all the interpretations of the song—like he absorbed all of these elements, and emerged with a comprehensive and unassailable version.

"I noticed that when Leonard was singing it this last time I saw him, it was like he was trying to take it back," said Bono, "trying to remind us of the irony, the humor in it, take some of the portentousness out and bring it back to his original humility, bring it back to earth. He performed it like Lucky in *Waiting for Godot,* taking off his hat.

"It had all of its richness without any robes, any grandeur. He was wrestling it back to earth, like one of Blake's angels that's tethered to the ground. That song is not meant to be up with the angels—the thing to watch for is when people make it too lofty."

The tour rolled on—in 2010, Cohen did a final, fifty-six-show run, starting in Zagreb, Croatia, and finally winding up in Las Vegas in December. Cohen's 2009 tour earned a reported $9.5 million. The 2010 dates sold 375,000 tickets and took in an astonishing $40 million around the world, making it one of the thirty biggest tours of the year—ahead of such artists as Elton John, Alicia Keys, Carrie Underwood, and Rod Stewart, and with an average nightly gross higher than those of John Mayer and Justin Bieber.

Interest in Cohen also led to the release of some revelatory historical material. His tense, moving 1970 appearance at England's Isle of Wight Festival was issued as a CD and a DVD. A controversial, long-out-of-print documentary of his 1972 tour, *Bird on a Wire,* was also given a DVD release; the movie is built around two concerts in Israel at which an exhausted Cohen tries to maintain order amidst security and technical disasters.

Following the Kelley Lynch debacle, the septuagenarian Cohen had put himself back into financial security. What's more, by the end of the tour, his show included four new songs, and he indicated that he had another seven or eight written, with plans to return to the studio early in 2011. If he would never be able to reclaim all of the money due for the latter-day success of "Hallelujah," he was certainly able to use its popularity wisely, and keep looking to the future.

In fact, by this time Cohen himself had started expressing some "Hallelujah" fatigue. He told the Canadian Broadcasting Corporation in 2009, "I was just reading a review of a movie called *Watchmen* that uses it and the reviewer said, 'Can we please have a moratorium on "Hallelujah" in movies and television shows?' And I kind of feel the same way."

Ironically, this divisive adaptation of the revered, disturbing graphic novel was one of the very few soundtracks to use Cohen's recording and not Buckley's. And the *Watchmen* scene scored by the song, in which two former superheroes who were unable to perform sexually in their civilian clothes put on their costumes and make love, may not work dramatically (it was, in fact, a sequence that some reviewers singled out for attack), but in some ways, it gets at the song's uncertain muddle of spirituality and eroticism more precisely than most of the more glib usages.

Cohen's own objections notwithstanding, in 2009, when both Alexandra Burke's and Jeff Buckley's versions of the song were riding high on the charts, and Leonard Cohen's tour was conquering the world, Martin Bandier, the chairman and CEO of Sony/ATV Music Publishing, spoke to *Billboard* about "Hallelujah." At a time when record sales and revenues had plummeted, publishing looked like the best bet in the music business, since these companies profited from every soundtrack placement, cover, and commercial use of a song.

"This is one of those songs that we very carefully guard in terms of how it's used and who it's licensed to for product endorsement and anything like that," Bandier said. "I think that there are wonderful things that are out there where the song can be used. We're not against it, but I do think that we carefully watch it."

"To put it in today's parlance," said Bandier, "it's protecting the brand. 'Hallelujah' is a brand."

CHAPTER ELEVEN

The children of *Shrek* were growing up. And as they continued to encounter "Hallelujah" in the music of the bands they liked, and in the foreground and background of the television shows they watched, they were also hearing it, and singing it, in settings closer to home. The impact of the song was extending beyond music culture, and into culture itself. It's quite remarkable, in fact, how often "Hallelujah" has figured into the everyday lives of my own friends and acquaintances, as I discovered once I started casually asking around.

Brian Glickman was working as a counselor and music director at North Star Camp for Boys in Hayward, Wisconsin. In the winter of 2005, one of the camp's other counselors, Alex, became stricken with encephalitis during a vacation in Hawaii. He was in a coma at one point, and remains in a wheelchair today.

Glickman loved Buckley's "Hallelujah," and, having

learned it at home, decided to play the song at the 2006 pre-camp staff show and dedicate it to Alex. "I wasn't sure I would make it through it," he said. "I started to strum the chords and either closed my eyes as I sang or looked at the floor. I knew that if I made eye contact with any of my friends, I would most likely start to cry."

When he looked up, he saw a counselor named Jake curled up in a corner of the room, weeping. "That actually made me smile, if only because Jake was a big, macho football player and I had reduced him to a puddle of tears," Glickman said.

After that night, he was asked to perform the song at the first campfire of the season, and then it became a staple of the summer (minus the second, "kitchen chair" verse, which he "didn't think would fly with the directors"). Glickman sang "Hallelujah" all the way through the season, including on the last night of camp, which was "request night," and each time, the kids all sang along.

Camp sing-alongs marked one rite of passage, but "Hallelujah" had also started to appear in another new, more formal context: Increasingly, the song was being used in religious ceremonies—weddings and funerals, but also regular services, across the Judeo-Christian spectrum. If, as k. d. lang pointed out, we live in a time when people are looking for spiritual connections that feel authentic, "Hallelujah" was one of the conduits providing an opportunity to make that link.

Reverend Sandy Scott of St. Paul's Presbyterian Church in Saskatchewan singled out two Canadian artists, Cohen and Sarah McLachlan, as the most frequent additions to his congregation's events. "When planning worship services . . . more and more are requesting popular songs to be used in place of hymns," he said, while noting a bit skeptically that "the music is written from the perspective of human experience, and less as a reflection on scripture and the work of the Holy Spirit in the world."

With Cohen's work, though, the Reverend pointed out that there was a fit that went beyond a fuzzy spiritual feeling. "The music and poems of Leonard Cohen were not written for the synagogue or the church, and he does start with human experience, but some of his poetry and music engages in an exchange or conversation with scripture." Noting that in Jewish tradition, the Cohen surname indicates a member of the priestly class, Reverend Scott went on to offer his thoughts on the reasons that people wanted to bring "Hallelujah" into the church.

"The hallelujah being declared is not from a confident and victorious believer who has seen the light, has the answers to everything, and is entitled to God's blessing and salvation," he said. "I think it is a song of praise for those who have experienced loss, pain, and sin in life and yet still believe God can reconcile and even redeem the things that we cannot.

"There are days, I am sure, when you and I and even the great King David could only muster a cold and lonely Hallelujah. It may be that the cold and lonely Hallelujah is a turning point that marks our salvation, because we know only God can save us from some of the situations we find ourselves in. The cold and lonely Hallelujah is a surrender to the mystery and backhanded glory of God."

Hartwick College professor Lisle Dalton explains that there is extensive precedent for bringing popular song into worship. Churches have used songs from musical theater dating at least back to Gilbert and Sullivan, and a few contemporary hymnals actually include songs by the likes of Rodgers and Hammerstein and Andrew Lloyd Webber. "There are lots of other genres that have been 'baptized' as well, including rock, folk, country, and even punk," said Dalton. "That 'Hallelujah' has biblical allusions is probably seen as a bonus, but it's not absolutely necessary in this type of music."

Of course, the specifics of the "Hallelujah" lyric, and the options it allows, do seem to lead the song to places other compositions can't go. Consider this post, which Dalton found on an online wedding forum thread from someone with the username "winter bridezilla":

"I love hallelujah, fab song and would love it sang at the wedding . . . but maybe a sensored [sic] version if one exists. what do people think? totally inapprorpiate [sic] or would be lovely. . . ."

Responses ranged from people saying that they had sung it in church but took out anything "offensive" to a suggestion to play the instrumental of the verse and just sing the chorus. But, Dalton points out, other religious usages have stuck with the original lyrics, believing that they are obscure or ambiguous enough to lend themselves to varied interpretation.

"You could look at the more sexually suggestive lyrics, like 'I remember when I moved in you' in a nonsexual way—'moved' connoting an emotional change of heart or a spiritual change," he said. "I'm sure there are many congregations that even like that the song has multiple layers, and appreciate Cohen's efforts to link his own personal struggles to biblical characters and themes."

Rabbi Ruth Gan Kagan of Jerusalem's Nava Tehila synagogue has utilized the song in a number of different ceremonies. Her daughter chose to sing it at her bat mitzvah. ("She was singing about the heartbreak of a sixty-year-old man!" Kagan said with amusement. "But it was her choice.") A distant relative of Kagan's asked her to officiate at his wedding. The bride and the groom were both musicians, and didn't want a religious ceremony, but wanted "a certain enchantment." She suggested they start with a *niggun*—a mostly wordless, hummed melody—but they couldn't agree on what to sing.

She tossed out the idea of using "Hallelujah," and they "lit up like Hanukkah candles," she said. "For a secular Israeli crowd, this is like a holy chant. And they had four hundred guests, young and old, and everybody was singing."

The most codified use of "Hallelujah" Rabbi Kagan has attempted came when she introduced "Hallelujah" into the Yom Kippur service at Nava Tehila in 2009, a month after Leonard Cohen played a concert in Tel Aviv to benefit Palestinian and Israeli peace groups ("everybody was still under his spell," she recalled). Kagan, a lifelong Cohen fan, had previously used his "If It Be Your Will" as a Day of Atonement prayer.

"In the beginning of the Kol Nidre service, we say three times 'Al da'at ha-Makom'—a prayer saying we hereby make it permissible to pray with the wrongdoers," she said. "It doesn't mean there are some black sheep and they can come, too. It means bringing our whole self, including the wrongdoer inside ourself, even the piece that maybe doesn't want to be there or doesn't believe. 'Hallelujah' is not a hymn of the believer—it's a hymn of the one who is full of doubt, a hymn of the heretic. In Hebrew, the word heretic shares the same root as kippur, 'atonement.' So the song is an opportunity to bring that heretical part in—not just the one who is ready for repenting, but the part that is doubting."

Asked how she can reconcile this skeptical sensibility, and the language of Cohen's song, with the more traditional aspects of the High Holidays, Kagan answered immediately. "I don't want to reconcile!" she said. "The whole reason of bringing it in was that it *doesn't* reconcile.

"Yom Kippur is not an easy day. That confusion is good, and it works better to admit that. Maybe I'm not sure I want to ask forgiveness—and who from, anyway? We should bring the poems that reflect this more complex relationship with God into the service. This is not the only poem of Cohen's with this question, but it also has that 'Hallelujah,' which is a good answer.

"One young man who used to be religious came to the service, and it was the first time he came to Yom Kippur after ten or fifteen years. He told me, 'I was sitting there all in knots, thinking, This isn't the place for me, why did I come? And as soon as you started singing "Hallelujah," I relaxed. I thought, There's room for me here.' "

Kagan said that people have told her to edit or alter the lyrics, but she refuses to do it. "People say it's too dirty for children, but I prefer to give honor to the words—otherwise don't sing them at all," she said. "I saw a rabbi who set the words of Psalm 150 to the melody of 'Hallelujah,' but for me that's a little kitschy. I don't like to kill that heretical message of the poem. I don't want to be tricked into believing that he's saying everything is going to be okay."

Taking the opposite approach, Helen Hamilton led the congregation of the Holy Trinity Church in Jersey, the largest of the Channel Islands off the coast of Normandy, France, in a rendition of "Amazing Grace" set to the melody of "Hallelujah." In the sermon that followed, she explained that she always felt the tune was "crying out" for Christian words.

"Don't get me wrong," she said, "I love Leonard Cohen's words, set in the Old Testament from David's point of view . . . but it's not the whole story, is it? Leonard Cohen obviously didn't find it enough. He converted from Judaism to Buddhism and spent five years in a Buddhist monastery. No wonder he talks about broken, cold, and lonely hallelujahs."

So Hamilton (whose sermon also stated her fondness for Buckley's version of "Hallelujah") married the song's melody and chorus to the immortal lyrics of "Amazing Grace," and in doing so, she presented the salvation offered by Jesus Christ as a counter to the idea that "it all went wrong." That, for Hamilton, completed Cohen's narrative—"we will be able to stand there, at the end of time, with nothing on our lips but hallelujah. Not through anything we have done, but through amazing grace."

Looking at these different usages of "Hallelujah," one thing that stands out is not only how the song remains so open to interpretation and flexible in meaning and construction, but also how easily it fits into services and celebrations

of multiple faiths. Though the song's language, and the chorus itself, derive from specific sources, the words composed
by the Jewish Buddhist travel easily from church to synagogue, and from wedding chapel to graveyard.

"There's a universality to the word *hallelujah*," said Cantor Jen Cohen of Temple Beth Sholom in Cherry Hill, New
Jersey. "Someone gave me the advice long ago that whenever
a Jewish clergy person or choir is called upon to participate
in an interfaith service, any prayer or psalm or song with
'hallelujah' in it will always work. People are overjoyed to
share that word with other faith traditions."

Cohen chaperones a trip to Israel every year with a crop
of tenth-graders. In 2010, the group visited the underground
City of David water tunnels. Outside the tunnels, they had
a view of the crowded rooftops of East Jerusalem, and their
guide said that this could have been the very spot where
King David saw Bathsheba "bathing on the roof." Picking
up on the reference, Cohen started to sing "Hallelujah,"
and all of the kids joined her for the choruses. ("Whatever
one thinks of the Hebrew Bible and its status as the greatest
fiction ever," she said, "I love when those moments happen
in Israel.")

The song turned up at the wedding of Amanda Palmer
to superstar fantasy writer Neil Gaiman (*The Sandman,
Coraline*) on the day after New Year's 2011. The event took
place at the San Francisco home of writer Michael Chabon,

with guests including Armistead Maupin and Daniel Handler, best known for the children's books he's written under the name Lemony Snicket. After a takeout Mexican dinner, everyone started to drink and sing.

"Pretty much everyone except the kids was drunk," recalled Palmer, "and someone suggested, 'We've got to sing "Hallelujah." ' It's a great party song—but it's not a 'beginning of the night' party song, it's an 'end of the night, everybody's drunk, somebody's got a guitar, that's the song you sing' song. And because I know that, or because I don't, I don't always remember every verse. So I started playing the chords on the piano and Daniel Handler had an accordion, and we all folked it up and played it, and it was actually Michael Chabon's teenage daughter that remembered the first line of every verse."

Another couple that used the song in their wedding was Mirjam van Emden (my own sister's husband's sister—my sister-in-law-in-law?) and her husband, Daniel Elzas, who made it the first dance when they were married in Amsterdam in 2011. Like many people his age, Daniel first heard "Hallelujah" in *Shrek,* and when Mirjam was an exchange student at the University of Michigan in 2004, the choir of the local Hillel performed it. "In my ears, they were able to keep so many musical layers in there with just their voices," she said.

The decision to include the song at the wedding had

more to do with the melody than with the words, though Mirjam's own interpretation of the lyrics also made it feel relevant to the occasion. "It talks about unevenness in a relationship," she said, "especially about lack of communication, which I think exists in certain periods and to a certain extent in every relationship, even though you try to do your best together. By the end, the communication seems to revive, even if it doesn't seem to repair the relationship. The word *hallelujah* seems to symbolize the connection between the two and the times when it was or it will be better— a word of hope, future, dreams, and wishes, which are quite appropriate to a wedding."

Not that the song had entirely transformed into a song of celebration. In September of 2005, newborn Danielle Burigsay died on her fifth day of life. Her parents made a video for the memorial service at Santos-Robinson Mortuary in San Leandro, California, with accompanying music including Jeff Buckley's "Hallelujah."

"I don't really know why I picked it," said Danielle's mother, Ann Burigsay. "I honestly never really knew what the song was even about. The song has always seemed sad but powerful, and has an impact on my heart that I can't explain. Maybe it felt like a final send-off and a blessing? For me, I guess the melody and the chorus is what I respond to most, not trying to decipher or make sense of the lyrics."

This kind of use might have seemed logical when "Hallelujah" was serving as the anthem of sorrow and romantic ache popularized through *Scrubs* and *The West Wing*. At that time, in fact, it would have been very difficult to imagine choosing the song as part of a celebration or happy occasion. In time, however, it became clear that "Hallelujah" could convey different moods than those established by the intimacy and longing that defined Jeff Buckley's performance.

Yet as "Hallelujah" proved itself to be just as powerful expressing triumph as it was expressing loss, or desire, or perseverance, history has seen this ambiguity turned into the song's great strength. Those who want or need it to serve as a hymn, a balm, can find that sense of soaring grace, and those who respond to its sense of struggle and confusion can present that as the song's backbone. There is no "right" way to sing "Hallelujah."

As time went by, those listeners who had discovered "Hallelujah" earlier in its existence now had more complex relationships to the song. Many old-school Cohen and Buckley fans felt that it had been corrupted by all the licensing and *Idol* worship. Others found that the journey the song had taken was something that mirrored their own experiences.

Back in the early 1990s, James Talerico was in a bad way. He had graduated from college and was spending his time traveling, drifting through Europe and the Middle East. At one point, he wound up on the Greek island of Santorini, where he fell in with a group of friends, including another American named Todd, a guitar player who was busking and tending bar in the town of Thera.

Todd was "committed to what he felt were the great unrecognized songwriters of American music," said Talerico, who is now the creative director for a digital advertising agency in New York City. Todd would play his friends tapes of Tom Waits, Rickie Lee Jones, Bob Dylan B-sides, and a Canadian singer Talerico was unfamiliar with named Leonard Cohen—who, as it happens, had lived for a number of years on one of the Greek islands himself.

Todd would tend bar and play these cassettes and Talerico would drink, and then closing time would come, and their friends would usually all wind up hanging out on the porch of the house Talerico was renting on the town's main drag. "We would sit out there, smoke a lot of black hash, and listen to music," he said.

Todd played Cohen's "Hallelujah" over and over. Talerico thinks they were listening to a live version from a bootleg recording. "That song had percolated up in his consciousness," said Talerico. "Particularly the opening verse—this idea of a secret chord, of there being some transcendent element, if only you could hold on to it."

"Hallelujah" began to lodge itself in Talerico's brain as

well. "My initial relationship to the song was kind of mo-
rose. It wasn't the most optimistic part of my life. I drank
a lot, I did a lot of drugs—and it was actually a lovely place
to do it, you're in the sun—but it was a hard slog night after
night, and I wasn't very healthy emotionally. And listening
to it again and again, it was like a sad kind of testament—it
felt like he was talking about no matter how hard you tried,
it almost didn't matter. The 'secret chord,' 'you don't really
care for music'—there were all of these overtures to our
mangy little efforts at something transcendent, and it falling
or not holding fast, which felt pretty consistent with where
I was at."

Talerico made a tape of his own favorites from Todd's
collection, including "Hallelujah," and he listened to it
through the rest of his travels—through Italy, concluding in
London before returning to the U.S. the following year. "It
was part of my soundtrack of being alone and pessimistic,"
he said.

Talerico eventually made his way to New York, moving
to the East Village and reconnecting with a musician friend
he had met along the way. His friend told him about a young
singer named Jeff Buckley, whom he had seen play at Side-
walk Café, a little club in the neighborhood. Other friends
were talking about Buckley, too, and about the wide range
of covers that he performed, including the Leonard Cohen
song that Talerico liked.

Things had begun to turn around for Talerico. He started out working at a job that he hated, but then he met someone with whom he would start a new business. He also met the woman he would eventually marry, though she was still with someone else. "I was still coming out of those years of not feeling right, but I had just started to gain some momentum," he said.

Talerico went to the late, lamented Tower Records store on Broadway and East Fourth Street and bought *Grace*. He heard Buckley's version of "Hallelujah"—the young singer's impossibly expressive, angelic voice heightening the sense of sensuality, with some different verses, and some that he recognized from the live Cohen bootlegs—and now he picked up on something different in the song.

"It felt like being able to have that aspiration, to be able to commit yourself to transcendence—whether it's recognized or not, and no matter how small it was—that was beautiful. And I think that actually came through Buckley's interpretation, which is heavenly, like he carries you up with it.

"Cohen gave me this really solid baseline on which I settled a lot of these grievances against the planet," Talerico continued, "and it reinforced a sense of pessimism that I had. Buckley just turned it upside down for me." The new recording of the song became his "personal anthem" through an exhilarating, tumultuous time, as he began dating music publicist Shawn McCormack and, just three months later, married her.

Each of the two different renditions of "Hallelujah" came to define a formative moment in this one life. "I love having these two different relationships with this one song," said Talerico, "particularly because each one really was where I was as a person—like, if I were in a more optimistic place, might I have found the hopefulness in Cohen's version initially? Maybe I would have. Within the lyrics there are so many opportunities to go either way—the Samson and Delilah reference, the 'cold and broken Hallelujah'—is there hope in there, is it death, is it despair? You're allowed to bring to it what you will. But it took Jeff Buckley's glorious voice to bring it out to me, and for me to be open to it at the same time.

"You know the end of [T. S. Eliot's 'The Love Song of J. Alfred] Prufrock'? He's like, 'I've heard the mermaids singing . . . I do not think that they will sing to me'—that despair, that's really consistent with how I heard 'Hallelujah' in the beginning. It was like, there's something there, and it wasn't for me, and all my aspirations toward it were meaningless. But then, with that soaring finish that Buckley puts on, it became something else. It could be cold, it could be broken, your hair could be cut off, but maybe there is a little bit of it for me."

When Talerico got married, the understanding was that

he and Shawn were not going to have children. As time went on, though, they started to reconsider. "We had all of this love," he said, "and we felt we had enough love for another human being." Conversations, first casual and then less so, naturally turned to what they might name a baby, and Talerico had an idea. They could call her Hallelujah.

"I was like, 'Wouldn't that be brilliant? We could take all of that joy and put it into this name.' And Shawn laughed; she was like, 'Oh, my God, don't do that to your child.' " But Talerico held on to the idea, and kept it at the bottom of the list of potential names. Shawn got pregnant and they learned that the baby would be a girl, which reduced the options, and down to the end, there were just a couple of names left in play—and Hallelujah was still one of them. The father-to-be would play the song to the baby growing in his wife's belly.

Shawn had a very difficult pregnancy and was bedridden much of the time, but on August 8, 2001—in between the release of *Shrek* and the events of September 11—a new person arrived at the birthing center at St. Luke's Hospital. "The baby comes out and I catch her and I hold her up, and she's slimy and gross and bloody, like a little pterodactyl," said Talerico. "The nurse leaves, and I'm like, 'Well, what do you want to do?' And Shawn said, 'Let's call her Hallelujah.'

"It was the only thing that we felt was representative of

the experience. We thought it was such an incredible thing that we had found each other and brought this life onto the planet, and we never thought we would. I never thought that I would meet the love of my life and marry her and she would give birth to this beautiful, beautiful piece of life. And the only thing that I could think to name her was this word, and it was tied to my own transformation, and it came along with the transformation of how I looked at the song."

When they wrote the name down on the birth certificate form, the nurse asked if they were sure. "I was like, 'Yes, I'm really sure,' " Talerico said with a laugh.

They brought the baby home the next day. Talerico had kept the Buckley album cued up in the CD player just in case. They laid her in the bassinet and played the song.

At that moment, he said, "she became the embodiment of this idea, this little tiny hope that I had. So, in a way, my daughter functions as my daughter and this human and this great personality, but she also functions as a symbol. The verse about the 'cold and broken Hallelujah'—cold and broken, but still beautiful and transcendent—she kind of took it all on in this human form."

Hallelujah Talerico is now eleven years old. She usually goes by the name Lulu. She plays the guitar, and every once in a while, if her father asks really nicely, she will sing the song that gave her her name. Her own favorite version of "Hallelujah" is not performed by Leonard Cohen or by

Jeff Buckley, but by a Bulgarian-born artist she found on the Internet named Geri X.

Talerico said that reaction to the name tends to be all or nothing. "People love it, they think it's the most beautiful thing, or they're just aghast that we would do that to a child—that maybe it's too much weight, too much to handle for a child's name." He does note that it tends to get an enthusiastic response from clerical workers and office administrators, which has helped the family navigate the New York City public school system.

His daughter's own relationship to her name changes. "There was a while when she wanted to change her name to, like, Joan," he said. "Now she's playing with different nicknames—she said that when she goes to middle school, she wants to call herself Hallie. But I do love it when she introduces herself as Hallelujah. It's a rare occasion. But when she does, it's just great to hear that word coming out of her mouth."

CHAPTER TWELVE

In 2010, the "Hallelujah" brand was thriving. The song was everywhere.

On January 22, ten days after the catastrophic earthquake in Haiti, MTV Networks produced the all-star telethon "Hope for Haiti Now: A Global Benefit for Earthquake Relief." The musical lineup was pop royalty, top to bottom: Bruce Springsteen, Shakira, Dave Matthews, Taylor Swift. Bono and the Edge teamed up with Jay-Z and Rihanna in London; in Los Angeles, Kid Rock, Keith Urban, and Sheryl Crow joined forces. All the performances were made available for download on iTunes immediately, and between pledges and sales, the event raised north of $60 million to aid in the relief efforts.

At this point, it was probably inevitable that "Hallelujah" would make an appearance, but it was still a bit of a surprise when a close-up of fingers on a piano pulled back to reveal

Justin Timberlake beginning a slow and prayer-like perfor-mance of the song. With his friend and collaborator Matt Morris playing acoustic guitar and singing harmony and Charlie Sexton (a longtime member of Bob Dylan's band, among many credits) adding electric guitar washes behind them, it was more ragged and more powerful than anything you might expect from the former 'N Sync-er. It was the bro-ken hallelujah in full force.

In a phone call during a break on a movie set, Tim-berlake (who grew up in Memphis) explained that he is a "huge" Jeff Buckley fan: He named his dog after the singer, and he and his friends would sometimes go down to the spot on the Mississippi where Buckley drowned to try to retrace his final footsteps. He has messed around with "Hallelu-jah" at home, on guitar and piano, "a million times," and he often uses it when he's making films. "If a scene is moody or haunting, I'll listen to it in between takes."

Timberlake batted around a few ideas with Morris when the producers of the Haiti telethon called and asked him to participate. "Matt had a version of 'Help!' by the Beatles that was just unbelievable," he said, "but 'Hallelujah' be-came the front-runner because I started toying around with modifying the voicings on the piano." By altering the con-struction of the chords, Timberlake stumbled on a sound that shifted the mood of the song. "I found something that made it feel more uplifting," he said. "There were clusters of notes that made the choruses feel less descending and more rising.

"So I called them back and said that we had this beautiful version of 'Hallelujah,' but obviously it's so long, we had to cut it down to the three verses that we thought were appropriate for this moment. We only figured it out a day or two before—we were just kind of freewheeling it."

Once again, the take-what-you-want nature of the lyrics proved essential to the song's use, and success. "It was easier to find the verses that *shouldn't* be there—'remember when I moved in you,' that was way too intimate for something like this," Timberlake said. "But 'maybe there's a God above,' that seemed universally appropriate for what was happening, to question a higher power. The figurative nature of that seemed right. There are some dark verses in there, but to me it's not about retribution. It's ironic, in a dark and haunting way, and I thought we were able to give it a different context."

Despite the license to take liberties with the song, and his own interest in Leonard Cohen's work, the most intimidating part of "Hallelujah" for Timberlake was definitely coming up against Jeff Buckley's legacy. "We got there and were like, 'Is this sacrilegious? We might be committing suicide here—we really have to be careful right now.'

"I was nervous because I was so in love with Jeff's version," he went on. "But then I wonder how he felt, what he knew about it when he sang it."

Critics seemed unprepared for the poignancy of Timberlake's "Hallelujah"; *New York* magazine's website called it "the biggest surprise, and arguably the best performance of the night." The song shot up the iTunes chart, selling more downloads than any of the other telethon material, reaching the Number One slot over the weekend following the broadcast. Between YouTube and the MTV site, the video was viewed more than a million times during those few days.

If Timberlake put the song in front of young listeners, a few weeks later, it was their moms' turn to hear a new take. On February 10, immediately before the opening of the Winter Olympics in Vancouver, Oprah Winfrey featured the Canadian Tenors on her talk show. As the Tenors sang a harmonically immaculate, emotionally flat "Hallelujah," which they had recorded on their debut album, they were joined by a surprise guest—a surprise even to the group, who had to continue singing as they registered what was happening. Before the last verse, Celine Dion (another Canadian) strode onstage for a genuine "Oprah moment," and added some responses and filigrees to the final section that were relatively free of her usual histrionics. The audience, naturally, went bananas.

The opening ceremonies for the Olympics came two days later. A somber mood hung over the festivities: A Georgian luger had died earlier in the day during a training run. Following a slate of performances that included songs by such Canadian stars as Bryan Adams, Nelly Furtado, and Sarah McLachlan, the opening remarks were delivered, beginning with the president of the International Olympic Committee and ending with Michaëlle Jean, the governor-general of Canada.

And then came the chance for Cohen's song to reach the global masses. Wearing a white three-piece suit over a white shirt, k. d. lang was given a truly once-in-a-lifetime shot at "Hallelujah," which was presented, somewhat inexplicably, as a "song of peace."

"The producer asked me to sing it, and I couldn't fucking believe it," said lang. "That's like being handed a golden egg and saying, 'Do you want this?' But I said, 'The only way I'm going to do this is if I get to sing live,' which was either really stupid or really brave.

"I said, 'Well, am I going to get to sing the verses I want to sing?' And they ran it by the committee and they all said yes. They signed off, there was no back-and-forth—I mean, I don't sing the one where 'I moved in you' and stuff like that, so it's not that bad."

For the Olympics, lang said that in her choice of lyrics and in her delivery, she was looking for something that would translate around the world, a feeling that was "more of an empathetic reaching out of the hands to the universal selves, to embrace the fact that we all share the same emotional structure."

And what a delivery it was. lang's performance was stunning, a huge, bravura vocal that never lost the song's fundamental intimacy, never turned overblown. With the added pathos of the athlete's death that same day, this "Hallelujah" was a song of survival and hard-fought perseverance. While lang was singing, images of doves were projected on the stage floor, and then rose to the ceiling via columns to symbolize their release (which still wasn't enough to get her to include the lines "I remember when I moved in you / and the holy dove was moving too").

In the course of a few weeks, in front of two global audiences, the extremes of "Hallelujah" were defined. If Justin Timberlake was able to use the song to respond to a natural disaster, offering the confusion and pain of the broken hallelujah, k. d. lang had countered with the holy hallelujah, the universal feelings of struggle and reward that were also contained in the words.

The Olympic opening ceremonies were watched by a reported three billion people around the world. A single of lang's "Hallelujah" was released, which reached Number Two on the Canadian charts and Number 61 on the U.S. charts. More than twenty-five years after its unheralded release, a phenomenon that had already happened in Europe now reached North America—multiple versions of the song were simultaneously among the most popular recordings on the continent.

k. d. lang has sung "Hallelujah" at countless concerts, benefits, and ceremonies, but she doesn't hesitate when asked what her favorite performance was. "The Olympics really took it to a new level for me," she said. "Singing that song, in Canada, for the world—it's a pretty big, pretty beautiful opportunity."

Cover versions of all kinds continued to appear throughout 2010. Another vocal group, Celtic Thunder, weighed in with the blunt force implied by their name. Neil Diamond included a version on *Dreams,* an album of his "all-time favorite songs of the rock era," alongside selections by the Beatles, the Eagles, and Randy Newman. The album was self-produced (following two albums that Diamond recorded with mega-producer Rick Rubin), and reveals impressive restraint from "the Jewish Elvis"—"Hallelujah" in particular is given a simple arrangement, far from Diamond's usual theatrics, and even if his vocal can't fully resist some melodrama, it is nonetheless an effective reading.

Still, the heat started to turn up a bit on a simmering "Hallelujah" backlash. The review in England's *Guardian* newspaper described the song as "dulled by ubiquity," while acknowledging that Diamond "presented [it] in a new light."

Jake Shimabukuro, the young ukulele wizard, included the song on his 2011 *Peace Love Ukulele* record, where it acts as a kind of counterbalance to the album's other cover, his blistering version of "Bohemian Rhapsody." After the multitude of other "Hallelujah"s, it's invigorating to hear it played as an instrumental, to step away from the poetry and the voices and just listen to this stunning, simple melody.

"You can get the same satisfaction by singing it alone in your living room as you can onstage in front of an audience," said Shimabukuro. "It's a song that you sing for yourself, not necessarily for anyone else.

"With this song, people have such a strong personal connection that they can fill in the blanks—the more space you leave, the more they're going to fill in their own interpretation, their own lives, their own memories. And maybe that's what makes it so great as a live, performing song, because everyone in your audience becomes a part of your band, part of your choir or your orchestra, and it's because they're all bringing just as much to the song as you are as a performer."

If Justin Timberlake and k. d. lang articulated the extreme emotions that "Hallelujah" could still carry, the song's outermost musical possibilities may have been defined by Shimabukuro's solo ukulele on one side and opera superstar Renée Fleming's performance of the song as an orchestrated epic on the other. Fleming, one of the world's most acclaimed sopranos, included "Hallelujah" on her controversial album *Dark Hope*, on which she interpreted a carefully curated set of pop material that favored more obscure indie-rock songs by the likes of Death Cab for Cutie and the Mars Volta.

In an enormous photo studio along Manhattan's West Side Highway, where she was filming some promotional material for the album, Fleming explained how the song, which didn't exactly fit the project's concept, ended up on the album. "We did 'Hallelujah,' and it was just supposed to be a test," she said. "It came up somehow in conversation with David [Kahne, the album's producer] and he said, 'Just so I can get to know your voice, why don't you come in and do that, since you're familiar with it already?' So then everybody said, 'Wow, we like this, we want to keep it,' and eventually it morphed into a version where we decided to do all seven verses."

Prior to the sessions, Fleming was unfamiliar with most of the new songs she recorded, but she was well aware of the challenges surrounding yet another new "Hallelujah" at this point—and they felt familiar. "Obviously, it's a song that's been covered a lot, even recently, so it has to be interesting or there would be no reason to redo it," she said. "But that's also doubly true of classical music, because the same piece has been sung the same way for hundreds of years, so what are you going to bring to it?

"It's funny, I've decided 'Hallelujah' is kind of a Rorschach test for people, because everyone has a different reaction to it and to what I'm doing. I just sang it, and whatever came out was just natural and spontaneous and maybe that's the best thing, because there's kind of an enigma, both in the meaning of the words and the way Leonard Cohen said them, that catches people's attention."

The response to *Dark Hope* was largely muted. Though it was generally acknowledged that Fleming was attempting something far more ambitious than the usual "classical crossover" lite-pop travesties, most critics felt there was a lack of connection to the material. Fleming sang far lower than her signature soprano, and she had to get used to singing closely into a microphone rather than projecting to the back of the Metropolitan Opera House; producer Kahne likened the change required in her vocal power to "a Ferrari going through a school zone."

Though technically flawless, Fleming's "Hallelujah" is also bloodless. Losing both humor and sex, she finds neither the intimacy nor the communal power that the lyrics had repeatedly demonstrated. In the *New York Times,* Jon Pareles called the song's arrangement "too plush and fussy." (In a conspicuously snarky review of *Dark Hope* on NPR, correspondent Linda Holmes referred to "Leonard Cohen's 'Hallelujah,' which apparently everyone has to cover," and classical music critic Tom Huizenga replied, "Yes, even I'm working up a cover of that now.")

And while it was well-intentioned to record all seven

of the verses covered between the Cohen and Buckley versions of the song, the truth is that it doesn't work as well as either edit—it loses the focus that gives Cohen's rendition its spiritual questing and Buckley's its erotic intensity. It was certainly a mistake to sing Cohen's climactic "I'll stand before the Lord of Song" verse in the middle of the lyrics—as Bono's version had demonstrated, there's really no way to follow that. Nonetheless, Fleming thought enough of her "Hallelujah" to make it the only song from *Dark Hope* included on her 2012 anthology, *The Art of Renée Fleming*.

Fleming was shooting for the sublime, but "Hallelujah" also dwelled among the ridiculous. Scottish hausfrau-turned-*Britain's-Got-Talent*-sensation Susan Boyle included "Hallelujah" on her enormously successful 2010 Christmas album, *The Gift*. Given that the Jewish Irving Berlin wrote "White Christmas," perhaps it shouldn't be so shocking to see a song rooted in Old Testament imagery, composed by a Jewish Buddhist, embraced as modern Christmas material. It did, however, apparently require even more elision than usual of some of the lyrics, including cutting a verse in half for no discernible reason, so that the final line she sings before the concluding chorus is "I used to live alone before I knew you," which makes no sense at all.

Boyle slows every line to a pious, painful crawl, and adds a quivering melisma at seemingly arbitrary points. Irony, sex, confusion, experience—any of the elements that give the song its depth are simply erased, leaving verses that simply fill up the space between those Big Moment Choruses.

Naming Boyle's recording one of the "20 Worst Songs of 2010" in the *Village Voice*, Maura Johnston (an ardent "Hallelujah" tracker over the years) wrote that Boyle's "overly-enunciated, hollow singing of each word that doesn't mean 'praise God' makes you wonder if she was actually given phonetic instruction in the studio." Jon Bon Jovi put it more succinctly. "Who is the stupid fuck A&R guy who allowed that to happen? What executive who thinks he belongs in this business would do that?" (*The Gift* did reach Number One in the U.S. and the UK, though, and received a Grammy nomination—so in truth, Boyle's A&R executive probably got a bonus that year.)

In October, soft rock/R&B balladeer Michael Bolton filled in for an ailing Susan Boyle to perform the song, backed by a choir, on *Dancing with the Stars*, one of the highest-rated shows on television at the time, up there with *American Idol* and *Monday Night Football*. The biggest emotional charge here came from the fact that Bolton had previously been an unsuccessful contestant on the show—any lingering sense of spirituality fully gave way to pure, old-fashioned, show-business drama.

Bolton said that he was only vaguely familiar with the song prior to his stint competing on the show. "It was on [his dance partner] Chelsie Hightower's favorite tape to stretch and warm up to. She had a version of two guys doing an acoustic version. She played that a lot, and I started to listen a little more closely.

"Then, after I was off the show and back on tour, I got this weird call out of nowhere, saying that they had a cancellation from Susan Boyle. I was in South Dakota or somewhere. I said. 'Are you asking me to come back and sing on the show? I'd love to do that—that's what I should have been doing all along.' We flew out Monday, shot on Tuesday, and I flew back on Wednesday, and the only time I had the lyric sheet in front of me was right before the show. They had already cut the backing track with the children's choir and I was trying to see if I could match the key, to make everything easier. That was the first time I actually read the lyrics, and I've never seen or heard the same set of lyrics twice."

Bolton said that the best take he did was the first one, but because of a technical issue, they had to redo it. The version as it was broadcast—though *Dancing with the Stars* fans would presumably disagree—plays awfully close to parody. For Bolton, a singer prone to bombast (and self-aware enough to lampoon his own style on *Saturday Night Live*), the vocal is relatively dialed back, but it's still a big, clarion delivery. With applause breaking out at inopportune times in the lyric—either for couples in formalwear spinning and dipping, or for the appearance of a children's choir, or for the familiar notes of the chorus—the whole thing feels ridiculous.

Whatever one's own reaction to the clip, Bolton has certainly put some thought into the structure and meaning of the song. "I think of 'Hallelujah' as 'thank God,' when something phenomenal or life-altering happens that saves you," he said. "There's a positive power in that word, some sort of saving grace.

"When you get to 'I've seen your flag on the marble arch,' there's a kind of defiance, a shift that happens. I love that lyric; love and mercy aren't what you think they're about, it's not about waving the victory flag. It really makes it so human and humble."

After the *Dancing with the Stars* performance, Bolton kept "Hallelujah" in his repertoire. He sang it in Italy, in front of a full orchestra and children's choir at a Christmas concert in the basilica of St. Francis of Assisi, for broadcast on Univision in Europe, and he included a recording with "MB's Children's Choir" on the 2011 duets album *Gems*, alongside songs with the likes of Seal, A.R. Rahman, and Rascal Flatts.

Also in 2011, Bolton sang "Hallelujah" to close the "Ein Herz für Kinder" telethon in Germany. "I was thinking I should do a big vocal, a powerhouse hook, but they asked for this song," he said. "So I did it and people were crying and the cameras went to the face of the Princess of Monaco, with tears streaming down her face. The host, Thomas, is someone I've known for twenty years and wouldn't describe as the most emotional guy, he's crying. And they raised 14 million euros. It was an amazing finale, this song with a chorus that's lower than some points in the verse. It was one of the most powerful experiences I've ever had on stage."

You might think that after all of this exposure, the televised singing contests would start to leave "Hallelujah" alone. But it seems that for these shows, familiarity breeds opportunity; even after all of these appearances, use of the song only increased. A fifteen-year-old boy performed the song on the *Australia's Got Talent* television show, and made it all the way to the finals of the competition.

In the 2010 season of *American Idol*, "Hallelujah" turned up not once, but twice—performed first by Tim Urban, and then by eventual champion Lee DeWyze. At this point, in fact, conspiracy theorists started to posit that Simon Cowell had some financial stake in the song, and that was why he kept returning to it on his series; Cowell actually had to issue a statement that he has no special interest in the composition or its publishing rights.

Urban did the song in full contemplative mode—alone, with his guitar—and impressed the judges. Ellen DeGeneres, who served as one of the panelists that year, came out from behind their table and hugged him. But it would be DeWyze who, later in the season, used "Hallelujah" to propel himself into the *Idol* stratosphere.

In the summer of the following year, before *The Voice* and *The X Factor* had watered down the show's impact as the only singing game in town, *Idol* mania still ran sufficiently rampant that a line of overexcited fans with signs and T-shirts circled the block outside New York City's Gramercy Theatre when I met DeWyze in a downstairs lounge to talk about the song.

"We got to one of the final weeks and they were going over all these songs with me they were thinking about having me sing," said DeWyze. "I got to sit down with Simon Cowell in his trailer, and out of nowhere he was just like, 'What about "Hallelujah"?' Jason Castro had done it the year before, and Tim Urban did it that season, so when they picked it for me and I was like, 'Uh, guys, we did this already this year, and last year.' But Simon said, 'I want to hear your voice sing this song.' "

Once the selection was made, DeWyze started by listening to "probably eight different versions" of the song, and tried to come up with an arrangement that fit. "I really wanted to do something that was a little more me, put my spin on it," he said. "I went on the show and I had a little gospel choir with me, which was cool. It's a very waltzy gospel song."

He opened solo with his guitar, before a string section came in behind him. At the first chorus, a choir entered from backstage. By the second and final verse of this performance (the "marble arch" verse), a full orchestra had joined for a roof-raising finish. The judges called the rendition "unbelievable" and "stunning"; DeWyze expressed that he was initially a little skeptical of Cowell's choice, and thanked him for making the call.

Post-*Idol*, DeWyze has used the song as the encore in his concerts, experimenting with different combinations of verses. "My favorite is, 'I heard that there's a God above / but all I ever learned from love / was how to shoot at someone who outdrew you. / But it's not a cry that you hear at night'— all that. For me, it's like all of these things that are kind of bad are happening, and what that verse said to me is that your faith is going to come down to a broken plea to God."

After DeWyze's *Idol* performance, MTV.com ran a story titled "Why *American Idol* Needs to Retire 'Hallelujah' as Soon as Possible." The site's *Idol* correspondent, Kyle Anderson, wrote, "As songwriting goes, it's pretty close to perfect. But that's just the problem, as too many people are able to make it sound too good. . . . No performance moving forward will top [Jason] Castro's, but there will also never be a bad version of it. Singing 'Hallelujah' proves absolutely nothing."

Meanwhile, the "Hallelujah" train kept a-rollin'. On July 9, 2011, in Montreal, U2 played a section of the song as an introduction to "Where the Streets Have No Name," presumably in tribute to the author's hometown. They skipped it at the next show, in Toronto, but then kept this segment in the set for the final six shows of the record-setting 360° tour, including the concluding night, July 30, in Moncton, New Brunswick—ironically, the province where Cohen had launched his own tour.

Bono was uncharacteristically vague when talking about the decision to add "Hallelujah" to the set list. "Often how U2 works is that we do something by accident and if it connects, we'll try it again until it stops," he said. He noted that he's often turned to the word *hallelujah* over the years while searching for something to stabilize himself mid-performance. "Onstage, you have all kinds of distracting thoughts, sometimes dark thoughts—some of the brightest moments of clarity I've ever had have been onstage, and I've also had some terrible times performing, so I've always used that word if it seems to fit in a place."

The singer adds, though, that the position of "Hallelujah" leading into "Where the Streets Have No Name" is significant. "That song is one of those invitations where you say to the audience, 'Do you want to go someplace else? Shall we go there together?' I've even, in a way that some would find obnoxious, used the Psalms in that slot. So 'Hallelujah' is such a powerful thought there, such a great way in."

The following month, "Hallelujah" attained yet another landmark in its public use; the song served as part of the state funeral for Canada's New Democratic Party leader Jack Layton. Tens of thousands of people gathered in Toronto on August 27 for the public farewell to the country's much-loved opposition leader. Steven Page, the former lead singer of Canadian folk-pop band Barenaked Ladies, delivered a stark, dry reading of the song, backed by just a piano and cello, standing next to the flag-covered casket in Roy Thomson Hall.

Fitting for an iconoclastic figure like Layton, Page's powerful performance included an unexpurgated version of the lyrics, through all seven verses—ending with Cohen's concluding "even though it all went wrong" lines. It was a successful incorporation of both of the song's defining edits, but one that had been attempted surprisingly few times.

And just when it seemed the TV singing shows might give it a rest for a while, "Hallelujah" turned up yet again, on the semifinal show of the 2011 *X Factor* season. This time it was former burrito slinger Josh Krajcik alone at the piano, singing the song one more time, and moving Paula Abdul to tears.

Regardless of the burgeoning "Hallelujah" exhaustion expressed by some critics, of course, there's no going back.

Even if the film and TV placements stop and the flood of cover versions slows to a trickle—which is presumably inevitable, given the way pop appetites work—the impact and legacy of "Hallelujah" are now permanent. What the sprawling range of recordings and performances in 2010 and 2011 reveal is that its meanings are still shifting, still up for grabs.

Jeff Buckley's version established the meaning of "Hallelujah" for a while: His expression of romantic sorrow was solidified on September 11, 2001, and then disseminated through *The O.C.* and *House* and *One Tree Hill* and all the other TV dramas that knew they could put that particular emotion to work. But Susan Boyle's atrocious reading of the song in a Christmas context, or k. d. lang's soaring rendition to kick off the Olympic Games, or the song's appearance at my Yom Kippur services have as little to do with Buckley's interpretation as with Cohen's original. Listening to the song has turned into a public event rather than a private moment.

"Hallelujah" has persevered, mutated, expanded over the decades, accruing more and more attached memories through all of these interpretations and deployments. And as it was being presented by Leonard Cohen to adoring audiences in Tel Aviv and Moscow and Las Vegas night after night, it found yet another life. For now, at least, it has become a song of survival, a song of triumph.

CHAPTER THIRTEEN

S o what is it about this song?

Many dedicated followers of Leonard Cohen would argue that "Hallelujah" is not even this one songwriter's greatest achievement. "Dance Me to the End of Love," "Bird on the Wire," "Suzanne," or "Tower of Song" might all place higher in a poll of fan favorites. In a list of his favorite Cohen songs for the 2010 *Rolling Stone* "Playlist" issue, Rufus Wainwright didn't even put "Hallelujah" in his top ten. (Wainwright became even more deeply associated with Cohen when Lorca Cohen gave birth to Viva Katherine Wainwright Cohen, her daughter and Cohen's second grandchild, in 2011. Given Wainwright's touring schedule, Lorca is raising Viva, though Rufus and Rufus's husband visit as often as possible.)

The singers who have performed Cohen's work most frequently, such as Jennifer Warnes and Judy Collins, have tended to avoid the song. Until recently, most major magazine and newspaper profiles of Cohen didn't so much as mention "Hallelujah" when they reviewed the highlights of his career.

"I had no idea at all that this would become a historic song, and I'm still baffled," said Cohen's longtime engineer and producer Leanne Ungar. "Yes, it is an incredible song, but Leonard has written so many worthy songs. Why this one and not 'Anthem,' 'Ain't No Cure for Love,' 'In My Secret Life,' 'The Future,' or a dozen more?"

As we've seen, though, there are several elements that distinguish "Hallelujah" not only from Cohen's own body of work, but also from other crowning moments in pop music. If, as k. d. lang posited, people are hungry for spirituality in music—or, at least, are hungry for spirituality, which music is able to provide—then "Hallelujah" provides a sure-fire solution. In a world polarized by the black-and-white politicization of religion, the song offers a rare example of both reassurance and doubt. Obviously it has a recurrent prayerful element, but it's also evident in even the most superficial reading that the verses undercut any sense of simple, blind faith.

Unlike the breathtaking precision of some of Cohen's songs mentioned above, the lyrics to "Hallelujah" are confusing, slightly out of focus. Perspective shifts between verses. Images from different stories are crosscut, adding up to a mood more than a single coherent narrative. The effect is that, whether you hear it on your iPod or in a wedding ceremony, it can be as "religious" a song as you want it to be—a contemporary hymn or just something with a vague aura of holiness.

"Hallelujah" has continued to demonstrate its ability to fit the changing mood, and needs, of its listeners over time. In the alternative-rock '90s, gloom was chic. In the aftermath of September 11, survival and defiance were the order of the day. It's not surprising that the popular songs of each moment would reflect each mood. The exceptional thing this time is that one song was malleable enough to sustain for the whole ride.

Of course it helps that certain lines and even whole verses of "Hallelujah" are often simply jettisoned because they don't neatly line up with the message the singer is choosing to deliver. "I remember when I moved in you" clearly wasn't going to make the cut for Susan Boyle's version. "She tied you to a kitchen chair" doesn't fit all of the circumstances into which "Hallelujah" is now thrown, though it's actually surprising how often, and in which contexts, it is retained. Only have ninety seconds to put a song across on television? Slice it down to two verses and you still have something substantial to sink your teeth into.

Though Cohen has given his unspoken approval regarding whatever choices each singer makes, and indeed was modifying the song himself from the day it first came out, some argue that these alterations are a betrayal of the song. Others feel that the one-dimensional overuse of "Hallelujah" in formulaic TV dramas flattened the song's real impact in a way that can never be recovered.

In the end, though, isn't this what pop songs do? Once a track has been released, the public takes it and goes with it, or they don't. If it succeeds, it will resonate with fans in ways the songwriter may have never imagined.

An interpretation, by listeners or by another artist, can permanently alter the world's impression of a song, whether the composer likes it or not—"Born in the U.S.A." is still the most obvious example, but ask R.E.M. about "The One I Love" or Sting about "Every Breath You Take." This lack of control over how his songs were heard and utilized was one of the factors that literally drove Kurt Cobain to an early grave. This inherent ambiguity is only amplified for a song like "Hallelujah," which so adamantly refuses to connect all the dots.

When the Canadian Tenors appeared at the 2011 Emmy Awards and sang "Hallelujah" during the mandatory annual video tribute to television industry people who passed away during the year, it triggered the loudest "Hallelujah" backlash to date. Salon.com wrote after the Emmys that " 'Hallelujah' has become to music supervisors what 'At Last' is to lazy wedding DJs—cheap emotional shorthand for overwhelming spiritual feelings. And in the process, a beautiful, mysterious song has been turned into a tacky karaoke number, and become so common that it's been drained of its power to move." Writer David Daley added that the awards show montage "represented the victory of sentiment over meaning."

Kenny Mellman of the drag cabaret duo Kiki and Herb tweeted, "Just because Leonard Cohen's song has 'hallelujah' in it, doesn't mean that it is an appropriate song for the people who died tribute." (One of the responses to Mellman read, "I bet he regrets writing it now.") The Jewish online magazine Jewcy.com put it another way a few days later, on the occasion of Cohen's seventy-seventh birthday. To honor the event, they wrote, "We'd like to go ahead and ask people to stop doing awful covers of 'Hallelujah.' If possible, we'd keep it to the John Cale version, the Jeff Buckley one, and of course, the one by the master himself."

To the general public, though, these concerns didn't register, and the song seemed to score yet another bull's-eye: According to a press release the group's label issued, "Following the broadcast, sales of The Canadian Tenors' self-titled debut album soared over 2500%, landing them on the Top 10 of Amazon.com, while downloads of their single for 'Hallelujah' jumped an amazing 15,000%."

It's a bit surprising that no one has created a devastating "Hallelujah" parody yet. You would think that after all this time, and no shortage of ludicrous usages, there's an opportunity for comedy—maybe not the full "Weird Al" Yankovic treatment, but at least a gentle poke at its ubiquity. The few, inevitable YouTube spoofs include such choruses as "I Don't Like Tuna" or the Indian dinner celebration "My Lamb Bhuna" (food is the eternal go-to in the world of parody lyrics—just ask Weird Al). For now, though, the song still seems too sacred to spoof.

Not long after the Emmy awards, *Saturday Night Live* presented a sketch that showed the "In Memoriam" montage from the "Adult Video Awards," paying mock tribute to the fallen veterans in the porn industry. *SNL*'s Hal Willner said that there was talk of playing "Hallelujah" under the video, but it was voted down; instead, the show used the "inspirational" instrumental "Eclipse" by Jay Price.

If "Hallelujah" continues to swing back from Buckley's introspective, passionate take to a more open and inspirational reading, it will be interesting to see if Cohen's original lyrics will become more popular. Since the song's resurgence, the older artists have leaned toward his verses while the younger interpreters have stuck with the Cale/Buckley cut. But increasingly, it seems like what the performers of the song are striving for would be better served by a lyric that returns to the Lord of Song at the end, and offers a hallelujah of redemption rather than ending on a cold and broken hallelujah.

A quite beautiful version of the song was posted to the Christian website Godvine.com in April 2012 by three young women from North Pole, Alaska, named Jodi, Alana, and Morgan. Over a solo piano, but at a slower tempo than the one that propels the forceful attack of Cale's playing, they sing the first three verses associated with Buckley's recording, but then end on Cohen's, concluding "I did my best; it wasn't much" verse rather than the "how to shoot at someone who outdrew you" verse.

This cut makes for yet another layer of meaning in this song—focusing on the religious imagery, losing the doubt of "maybe there's a God above" and "I don't even know the name," but also adding an element of physical desire with the "love is not a victory march" line. Church choirs and other singers who respond to the song from a religious perspective should take note.

Its unknowable essence leaves "Hallelujah" wide open for interpretation, but crucially, it isn't vague or flimsy. For every line that might get dropped or glossed over, there are also several lines that always provide strong landing points, regardless of the singer or which version brought them to the song. "I've seen your flag on the marble arch, / but love is not a victory march" is a knockout no matter which message it is you're conveying, and even singers with a hazy understanding of the themes can find something in "all I ever learned from love / is how to shoot at someone who outdrew you."

The core of the song, its tense conviction, remains intact. There are good versions and bad versions, performances that are shallow and reductive and others that are revelations, but the magnificent thing is that the song stands strong and conveys undeniable feeling. The structure is rock-solid—it bends but does not break.

It is easily exploited, but it has evolved and adapted and become imbued with its own legacy. "Hallelujah" may not mean the same thing to Jon Bon Jovi and Justin Timberlake, to Rufus Wainwright and the various *American Idol* contestants, but the feeling it gives to each of them is genuine and rooted in the same fundamental concepts—spirituality, struggle, perseverance.

" 'Hallelujah' has a powerful mood," said Regina Spektor. "It's in the DNA of the song. It makes anybody feel amazing to sing it. So many songs you have to sing a certain way, or at the right emotional temperature, or they just collapse. This song is pretty much indestructible."

Glen Hansard believes that all of the covers and licenses and seemingly endless uses of "Hallelujah" have not diminished its power in any way. "There are very few perfect songs in the world, but it's really like a Hank Williams song—it's strong enough to withstand any treatment." Hansard said that he has sung it various times over the years with other people, but refuses to tackle it on his own. "It's such an incredible holy grail of a song," he said, "I just won't touch it."

Somehow, no matter how frequently it appears, "Hallelujah" has maintained its ineffable aura of cool. The combination of Leonard Cohen and Jeff Buckley—the brooding poet and the doomed golden boy, the visionary artist and the gorgeous prodigy, two icons of love and sex and mystery for multiple generations—is a magical pairing. Buckley's recording may not have registered with the public at first, but he was the ideal conduit to relay the song to the world. Even as both artists have become more familiar over time, identifying yourself as a fan of either singer, much less both of them, still holds an untarnished allure, an insider's hipness.

"Now it looks like it was so obvious, but there are lots of instances of people walking by something extremely special and not stopping to take note," said Bono. "Like with a great painting, like a Rothko—you can sit in that room in the Tate Gallery and just go, 'Well, there ya go, there's a nice feeling in here,' and not realize that this is a really important moment for you, and it was really hard-won by the artist to get here and find you. If you didn't stop and just think 'Okay, that's a great lyric,' you might miss the complexity. But in the end, this kind of thing just does come through."

David Miller of Il Divo thinks that it took time for the world to discover "Hallelujah" because it was so out of step with the era in which it was first created. "I think people just weren't ready to hear it," he said. "It's so in tune with an ethereal vibration, and the '80s was not an especially ethereal time. But then a bit of a shift happened, and people realized that maybe there's more to it than the house, car, computer, the things they own, and they were ready to hear different things.

"It's the same reason young people don't generally

go to the opera—they haven't lived enough. You have to feel that bruising of your heart to relate to the tragedy in opera, to these big, huge emotions on the stage. It's really for people who have lived forty, fifty, sixty years, and gotten to the point in life where you realize its brevity, and the importance of relationships and family. That's the fragile and tender place where songs like 'Hallelujah' come from." The world might have needed to catch up with "Hallelujah," but unlike opera, this "fragile and tender" core of the song resonates—and this was the magic of Jeff Buckley's interpretation—with youth as well.

"It's welcome proof that a great song will endure somehow," said Michael McDonald. "Even if it doesn't get the attention at first, it can capture the public imagination if the right artist can do it. Sometimes it takes the right combination to come along and make that connection."

"The song keeps coming up, and every time it's like it's brand-new," said Patrick Stump of Fall Out Boy. "It sounds new every time you hear it. It's a rare example of a true modern folk song. I was reading about 'La Cucaracha,' which is this folk nursery rhyme from the 1500s. There are hundreds of thousands of iterations, as a political song or a kids' song, it evolves and gets employed in all these different ways. That's how a lot of folk standards happen, but not a lot of modern songs do that."

The artists who are singing "Hallelujah," and not only

the ones you might initially expect, are usually very aware of its transformation. They know from experience that as the song has penetrated deeper and deeper into public consciousness, the personal baggage it gathers, the associations and affiliations, all have an impact on the way it is received.

"I think that the point of the song has maybe gotten lost a little bit along the way," said Lee DeWyze. "But it's one of those songs that really evokes emotions in people, whether they're religious or not. So many people say to me, 'I'm not a religious person, but when you play that song, I feel like you're connecting spiritually with everybody here,' or 'We had your version played at my father's funeral,' 'We had your version played at our son's baptism,' things like that. The song really means a lot to them."

Though Alexandra Burke was initially skeptical about performing "Hallelujah" on *The X Factor,* since her history-making success with it, she has learned firsthand both the power of the song and the contradictions it embodies. "My pastor recently asked me to perform 'Hallelujah' for New Year's, and I wondered what he was hearing in it," she said. "It is a dark, deep song, but because of that word, certain people will only notice and concentrate on that."

A composer like Leonard Cohen invites a very close consideration of his lyrics, but it's usually a melody that first connects with most listeners. So let's give the final word to the magical tune of this song. As befits Cohen's limited vocal range, "Hallelujah" is easy to sing. The song is built on a simple, gentle ascending and descending figure ("the minor fall, the major lift"). There's plenty of room for more gifted singers (Renée Fleming) to explore, but nothing to intimidate a less-conventional vocalist (Willie Nelson).

Listening to all those kids who filmed themselves for YouTube, or people singing it in languages I don't speak a word of, it quickly becomes apparent that unless a singer takes a genuinely risky approach to reworking the arrangement— see Bono and Susan Boyle, an odd couple if ever there was one—as long as he or she has any voice at all, it's very hard to make "Hallelujah" sound bad.

"It almost doesn't matter who's doing it; it's always nice to hear the song," said Norah Jones, who performed it once in 2003 at a charity event organized by Don Henley. "Yeah, it's overdone, but it doesn't really matter. The melody is so beautiful you just don't want to interpret too much."

"There's a lot of simplicity in the tune," said Jake Shimabukuro, "a lot of space, which for me as a player is inviting, because there's room to add things without compromising the melody or the spirit of the tune. There's a lot of space for contemplation, a lot of space for whoever wants to be a part of the song. And that's a very rare thing. A song like 'Hallelujah' takes you off the grid and gives you back some of that space that we're all missing in our lives."

And there is simply no getting around the power of that

chorus: one word, charged with centuries of meaning, delivered ironically or solemnly or both. It serves as a prayer, perhaps the great prayer of the modern age, regardless of one's relationship to God. One look at the tears streaming down the faces of a sea of kids singing along with Leonard Cohen at the Coachella Festival demonstrates the ability of this song, with one age-old word at its center, to transport listeners in a way that organized religion has largely failed to do for this generation.

"It's an amazing word to say," said Bono. "It's its own kind of mouth music just singing it. Praising God, Yah, Yahweh—it's a very powerful word, a big idea, and I've hung on to it very tightly over the years."

Are there any more places for "Hallelujah" to travel, any more worlds still left for this song to conquer? In March 2012, Leonard Cohen, flush with the success of the *Old Ideas* album, announced that he would be returning to the road, with a tour beginning in Europe in August and then heading to North America in the fall. Having traversed the globe from 2008 to 2010 as a means to secure his retirement, he decided that he didn't want to retire, after all—that he enjoyed the rhythm of touring and would like to give it another go.

"I hadn't done anything for fifteen years," he said at the London playback of *Old Ideas*. "I was sort of like Ronald

Reagan. In his declining years he remembered he'd had a good role. He'd played the role of a president in a movie. I kind of felt that somewhere I'd been a singer. Being back on the road reestablished me as a worker in the world, and that was a very satisfactory feeling." As of the most recent tour schedule, Cohen's seventy-eighth birthday falls in between dates in Istanbul and Bucharest.

The major piece left to be determined in Jeff Buckley's legacy is whether the biopic ever actually gets made. If there is still a project that could launch "Hallelujah" to yet another altitude in any sort of predictable way, the long-delayed film would be it. There's no way to know when or how or if it will be completed, but a draft of the *Mystery White Boy* script by screenwriter Ryan Jaffe reveals the song turning up at two key moments in the movie.

Early on, Buckley sings it in a Sin-é-esque café during a power outage. "A friend played me John Cale's version of this song and I fell in love with it," he says, "so I thought I'd play you my version." He gives a revelatory performance that the script describes as "a discovery for Jeff as much as the audience—he's got it."

Later in the film, he's annoyed by constant requests for the song, but plays it in Australia to honor drummer Matt Johnson's final show. He sits behind the drum and plays the beat with his foot and then starts the guitar part. He plays, Jaffe writes, "the saddest and loneliest version of the song you can imagine. Almost an anti-'Hallelujah.' " Buckley yells at the crowd to sing along: "You've been shouting for it all goddamn night. Sing it loud next time. Hit me. Hit me. *Hallelujah!*"

Maybe "Hallelujah" has plateaued; k. d. lang announced over lunch that she was going to quit performing it within the year. "Everyone's singing it, so maybe it's time to let it go," she said. "You know what it's like? It's like that scene in *Of Mice and Men* where the guy is petting the mouse and he kills it because he loved it so much. It's kind of like that."

Or maybe it will rise again, performed by an artist too unlikely to imagine (Willie notwithstanding, there hasn't been an authoritative country take on it), or at an event of great triumph or great tragedy, and reach a new audience in a new context that inspires more memories and associations. There's no way to see the future for this song, because there is no precedent for the trajectory it has already had.

A venerated creator. An adored, tragic interpreter. An uncomplicated, memorable melody. Ambiguous, evocative words. Faith and uncertainty. Pain and pleasure. A song based in Old Testament language that a teen idol can sing. An erotically charged lyric fit for a Yom Kippur choir or a Christmas collection. Cold. Broken. Holy.

"There is a religious hallelujah, but there are many other ones," Leonard Cohen once said. "When one looks at the world, there's only one thing to say, and it's hallelujah. That's the way it is."

AFTERWORD

As soon as you finish a book—especially a weird high-wire act like devoting an entire project to one song—the anxiety sets in. How soon will it be out of date? Will a new song suddenly rise up and seize the spot that "Hallelujah" holds in the culture? Will some new usage or placement forever alter the meaning of or associations with the song?

After *The Holy or the Broken* came out in late 2012, the story started to change the very next week. Hurricane Sandy had hit New York, New Jersey, and Connecticut on October 29, ravaging communities and basic services. A massive benefit concert to help restore and rebuild those areas was assembled at Madison Square Garden on December 12, with the event taking its name from the date—"12-12-12: The Concert for Sandy Relief."

It was among the greatest gatherings of talent for a rock show—or it might just have been, as Mick Jagger put it, "the largest collection of old English musicians ever assembled." The anchor acts included the Rolling Stones, the Who, Paul McCartney, Bruce Springsteen, and Billy Joel, though the bill was somewhat balanced out by young(er) guns including Alicia Keys, Kanye West, and Chris Martin of Coldplay. ("If you're going to donate tonight," said Martin, "think of a figure that matches the average age of the performers, and I bet we'll raise billions!") The nearly six-hour concert peaked with some collaborations that could only happen on a night like this. McCartney played with the surviving members of Nirvana. Jon Bon Jovi joined Springsteen for "Born to Run," and Bruce repaid the favor on Bon Jovi's "Who Says You Can't Go Home." Michael Stipe sang a lovely "Losing My Religion" with Chris Martin, and Eddie Vedder nailed the vocal in a duet with Roger Waters on Pink Floyd's "Comfortably Numb."

The "12-12-12" show also included numerous actors and comedians offering tales of heroic efforts in such devastated spots as Red Hook, Brooklyn; Breezy Point, Queens; and much of the Jersey Shore. Midway through the show, between the sets by Waters and Bon Jovi, Adam Sandler ambled onstage, backed by Paul Shaffer, who began playing a familiar, waltz-like melody. Known for his imitations and song parodies since his *Saturday Night Live* days, Sandler started singing "Hallelujah" in his familiar tuneless warble.

The lyrics, at first, were reverential enough: "The terror of the hurricane / The unforgiving wind and rain / New York, the world held its breath as the storm took it to you." When he hit the chorus, his play on the lyrics actually held close to the song's sense of battered uplift. "Hallelujah / Sandy, screw ya / We'll get through ya / 'Cause we're New Yorkers."

Sandler continued lamenting the storm's destruction, as well as the sorry recent fate of New York's sports franchises. As the verses went on, of course, he got ruder and more topical, with references to such local struggles as "Times Square losing all its porn," and "the mayor's ban on thirty-two-ounce Mountain Dew-ya."

As soon as Shaffer played the first notes, my phone started blowing up. The book had been out for all of eight days—was I okay with this desecration of the song? Being Adam Sandler, of course, soon enough his own gentle pokes at the lyrics had degenerated to "the lady who said she was a man right after she blew ya (sorry, that was just me!)" and, in the final verse's shout-out to New Jersey, "Turnpike Exit 13 stinkin' like poo-ya." I suppose it was at this point that my social media feed was filling up with people saying "Leonard Cohen won't be amused . . . and I'm not either," or "Terrible— as if I needed more reasons to hate Adam Sandler."

But you know what? Having spent the better part of the previous two years thinking about this song, I thought it was pretty damn funny. A Jewish comedian backed by a Jewish musician spoofing the work of a Jewish composer, transforming pain into humor, was a moment in the grand tradition of Lenny Bruce and Mel Brooks. Cohen himself was apparently cool with it, too—the night of the show, @LeonardOnTour ("the official Twitter feed of Leonard Cohen's Old Ideas world tour") tweeted "If we had to guess who would be singing Hallelujah at the #121212concert, we wouldn't have guessed Adam Sandler. But we dig it! #screwsandy"

Most of all, Sandler's "Hallelujah" was a testament to the composition's genuinely universal popularity—you don't stand up in front of hundreds of millions of viewers watching the broadcast of a mega-benefit concert and spoof a song unless you're pretty confident that most of them know it. And while the magical spirit of "Hallelujah," the meeting of prayer and sexuality its lyrics embody, may not benefit jokes about MTV's *Jersey Shore* reality-show atrocity or "the congressman who tweeted his dick," the song had taken more severe hits before—let's not forget Susan Boyle's Christmas record.

You might recall that just a few pages back, I wrote that it felt like the time had come for a "Hallelujah" parody, that its constant, somber presence seemed to present "an opportunity for comedy"—so here we were. If nothing else, it was confirmation of another quote in the book, this one from Regina Spektor: "This song," she said, "is pretty much indestructible."

Less than thirty-six hours later, though, another tragedy struck America. On the morning of Friday, December 14, twenty-six people—including twenty children between six and seven years old, and six adult staff members—were shot and killed at the Sandy Hook Elementary School in Newtown, Connecticut. It was the deadliest mass shooting at a primary or elementary school in United States history.

American citizens struggled, yet again, to make sense of the country's gun laws, and numerous marches and rallies were organized over the weekend. On Monday, NBC's singing competition show *The Voice* began its live finale week— but before the episode started, coaches Christina Aguilera, Adam Levine, Blake Shelton, and CeeLo Green, along with hosts Carson Daly and Christina Milian and a majority of the season's finalists, assembled on a candlelit stage. Each of them held a card with the name and age of a Sandy Hook victim, and together they sang "Hallelujah."

Any concern that Sandler's NSFW parody had punctured the song's impact was instantly gone. It was oddly fitting and slightly ironic that "Hallelujah," which had become such a staple of the televised singing contests around the world that it was verging on cliché, was able to utilize this format to serve as a powerful emotional outlet at a time of mourning. And the song turned up again at several of the memorial services for the fallen children. When it was needed, still, "Hallelujah" was there.

"Hallelujah" continued making inroads into other genres of music. Country stars LeAnn Rimes, Brett Young, and Wynonna all performed the song. The night after Leonard Cohen's death was announced, Keith Urban played it alone, with his acoustic guitar, at a Nashville concert; on his Facebook page, Urban posted the clip with the caption "RIP Leonard. And thank you for being a vessel of glory on high." He repeated the song in an "In Memoriam"–style medley at his annual outdoor New Year's Eve show in Nashville and posted another video playing it alone in his living room.

Modern-day outlaw Eric Church—who was named the Country Music Association's 2020 Entertainer of the Year, has won Album of the Year at both the CMA and Academy of Country Music awards, and has racked up seven Number One country singles—was getting ready for his 2016 appearance at Colorado's legendary Red Rocks amphitheater when Jeff Buckley's "Hallelujah" came up on his iPod. He decided he would take a shot at performing the song that night.

"I think it's the most brilliant song ever written," Church told filmmakers Dan Geller and Dayna Goldfine. "I know some people find sexual undertones in it, but for me, it's a spiritual song. I think that the great thing about the song, and what makes the song special, is you're able to attach so many different meanings from so many different people about the song. And they're all right. None of 'em are wrong."

Church describes his brawny, characteristically impassioned rendition of the song at Red Rocks—"I use to own this place before I knew ya," he shouted—as one of the most memorable moments in his career. Following that performance, he opened the rest of the shows on the tour by playing Buckley's recording, in full, with a single spotlight on a microphone stand at center stage. "Every night, the whole arena sings the song," he said. "I've never found anyone that has said, 'I just don't get the song' or 'I don't think it applies to me.' You can look at the number of artists that have covered the song, from all different genres of music, and you can tell pretty quick that it's just a timeless masterpiece.

"The thing about 'Hallelujah' is every time you hear the song, it feels like something big has just happened. You don't just hear the song and pass by it and move to the next song. When you hear 'Hallelujah,' it feels important."

"Hallelujah" may not be the easiest fit for country singers, but—given the genre's relationship to storytelling, emotional expression, and even religious themes—it makes a certain sense that it has tentatively found its way into the canon.

Another tradition that has somehow carved out space for the song is Christmas music. Though it was written, of course, by a Jewish Buddhist, it's hardly the first time that the composer of a yuletide favorite came from a different religious tradition; don't forget that "White Christmas" was written by Irving Berlin. The first direct association of "Hallelujah" with Christmas had come in 2010, when Susan Boyle included it on her holiday album *The Gift*, which hit Number One on both the *Billboard* 200 and the UK's Official Albums chart.

In 2015, the violinist and singer Lindsey Stirling, who came to prominence on YouTube, released a version that reached Number 81 on the Hot 100 and Number 21 on the Holiday 100 (which was introduced in 2011) the following year; that same year, German superstar Helene Fischer included the song on her hit album *Weihnachten*. (In 2014, a Christian rock band called Cloverton wrote some new lyrics—opening with the lines "I heard about this baby boy / Who's come to Earth to bring us joy"—and released the results as "A Hallelujah Christmas"; YouTube is littered with homemade covers of this version.)

Since 2016, however, the most popular version of "Hallelujah" on streaming services by far has come from a cappella superstars Pentatonix. The Texas-based quintet won NBC's singing competition show *The Sing-Off* and has gone on to win Grammys and release multiple gold- and platinum-certified albums. Their technically impeccable, emotionally generic recording, which was included on the 2016 *A Penta-

tonix Christmas album, has been streamed 350 million times in the United States since its release, according to Nielsen Music. It reached Number Two on *Billboard*'s Holiday chart and returned to the chart in 2018 and 2019. Their "Hallelujah" also went to Number One on the Austrian pop charts and hit the Top Five in Germany and Hungary.

Usually, Christmas songs have some kind of reference to the actual holiday—or, at least, are somehow adjacent to Christmas, with mentions of snow or winter or Santa Claus or something that would make the lyrics specifically seasonal. "Hallelujah" has none of those things. So why does it qualify or function as a Christmas song at all? *Billboard* asked Scott Hoying of Pentatonix about the song, and the most he could offer was that "when people hear it, they feel something."

Hoying went on to present the lack of holiday content as an advantage. "We were originally going to put Christmas lyrics in it," he said, "but we wanted to honor the poetic original. It's inclusive—people who don't celebrate Christmas can enjoy it."

Which is certainly true, though it remains odd that the song's ambiguous, imagistic lyrics about sex and spirituality, Jeff Buckley's "hallelujah of the orgasm," resonate with anyone as being synonymous with Christmas. (In a 2021 interview with the *Dallas Morning News*, Hoying admitted that "I don't totally know what the lyrics mean, but I'm pretty sure that song is about sex.") In 2019, Chris DeVille, a self-described "Christmas music fan," responded to the ubiquity of Pentatonix's recording with a rant on Stereogum .com titled simply " 'Hallelujah' Is Not a Christmas Song."

Though he described the group as "hokey and saccharine in the way only a cappella groups can be," he acknowledged that they are "great at singing Christmas songs." He noted that they had successfully shoehorned such "winter songs" as Fleet Foxes' "White Winter Hymnal," Kanye West's "Coldest Winter," and the Neighbourhood's "Sweater Weather" onto their Christmas albums, but called out their choices of the Mariah Carey/Whitney Houston duet "When You Believe," *Frozen*'s globe-conquering "Let It Go," and especially "Imagine" as holiday selections.

In sum, writes DeVille, "some of Pentatonix's Christmas bullshit I can begrudgingly abide." But their use of "Hallelujah" is a step too far. "Every time I listen to the Essential Christmas playlist on Apple Music," he writes, "this is exactly what happens: I'm cruising along enjoying the likes of 'Jingle Bell Rock' and 'Santa Baby' and 'It's Beginning To Look A Lot Like Christmas' and 'Santa Claus Is Comin' To Town,' and along comes this endlessly covered Leonard Cohen ballad about sexual ecstasy, crushing heartbreak, and existential doubt to make me spit out my hot chocolate. . . . It shares a certain reverent awe with certain carols and nativity ballads, but it constitutionally has nothing to do with Christmas. It exists on a different plane."

And yet, as we've seen over and over, "Hallelujah" assumes the meanings that listeners find in it. There is no logical reason that it should work as a Christmas song. But the devotion and power represented by that chorus, that melody, that feeling, somehow connect to people in this context. If it happened once, maybe it would just be a fluke or a novelty, but the fact that it has taken on this role at the holidays repeatedly speaks for itself. Like it or not, "Hallelujah" is also a Christmas song now.

Fifteen years after *Shrek*, "Hallelujah" returned to a prominent place in an animated feature film. *Sing* is a jukebox musical about a group of anthropomorphic animals who participate in a singing competition, hosted by a koala (voiced by Matthew McConaughey) who is trying to save his theater. Other characters featured the voices of Reese Witherspoon, Scarlett Johansson, and Seth MacFarlane.

The role of Meena, a teenage elephant with a glorious voice and paralyzing stage fright, was handled by Tori Kelly, who had been a semifinalist in the 2010 season of *American Idol* and a Best New Artist nominee at the Grammys. After the theater is destroyed through a series of mishaps, Meena returns to the rubble and sings "Hallelujah," inspiring the koala to rebuild and lead the way to a triumphant ending. *Sing* was a critical success and grossed more than $630 million worldwide—not the cultural juggernaut that *Shrek* was, but a major success that certainly introduced "Hallelujah" to yet another wave of young children.

At the movie's premiere at the Toronto International Film Festival, Kelly—who would also go on to sing "Hallelujah" for the "In Memoriam" segment of the 2016 Emmy Awards—was joined onstage by Jennifer Hudson in a performance of the song. (The deluxe edition of the movie soundtrack included a duet version by the two singers.) Hudson, like Kelly an *American Idol* alum, has displayed a special fondness for the song, performing it multiple times over the years and even, in 2017, posting a video of her seven-year-old son singing the song at home. After Leonard Cohen's death, she posted a statement saying that "Hallelujah" was "one of my favorite songs to sing."

Even Judy Collins—whose interpretations of Cohen's songs had been his initial introduction to the world back in the '60s—finally caved and recorded "Hallelujah" for the first time, as a duet with young singer-songwriter Bhi Bhiman on her 2015 album *Strangers Again*. "It was time," Collins told Geller and Goldfine with a laugh. "Give everybody a chance and then take a turn. It's a wonderful song, there's no question about it, and I always loved it. But it wasn't time ... yet."

Collins placed "Hallelujah" in the company of "Amazing Grace," "We Shall Overcome," and "Where Have All the

Flowers Gone?" in terms of its far-reaching, almost primal appeal, and recalled Cohen singing her "something like forty-five verses" to the song, confirming yet again his account of his struggle with the lyrics.

"It's probably the easiest [of his songs] to sing," she said. "It's a mysteriously accessible melody. And it's one word—when you hear the word 'hallelujah,' and you hear the melody that is so primary, it resonates in people's lives, like any kind of music that is hallowed in some way. And then it resonates forward with its discussion in the verses, which are also transformational.

"I always thought it was so wonderful," Collins continued, "his ability to cross all of the spiritual and religious paths and mingle them together. And in 'Hallelujah,' he brings it all together. It's a remarkable piece of work, and everybody picks up on it immediately. It's a revolutionary spiritual song."

Following the unprecedented success of the *Old Ideas* album, Cohen continued his streak of productivity. A world tour followed the record's release, continuing his three-hour-plus shows with essentially the same musicians, now dubbed the "Unified Heart Touring Band." Between August 2012 and December 2013, Cohen performed 125 shows, selling more than 600,000 tickets and grossing almost

$62 million. The tour's final stop was in Auckland, New Zealand, on December 21, 2013; Cohen closed, as usual in this set, with the Drifters' "Save the Last Dance for Me." It would be his final appearance on a stage.

But less than a year later, on September 19, 2014—two days before his eightieth birthday—Cohen was back with his thirteenth studio album, *Popular Problems*. A few of the songs had previously been performed onstage or published as poems over the years; once again, Patrick Leonard was enlisted as a producer and cowriter, though this time the band was largely different from the touring group. Reviews were certainly positive, though a bit less ecstatic (perhaps a bit less surprised?) than the reception of *Old Ideas*. The album went Number One around the world, from Canada to Portugal, reaching Number Five in the UK and Number Fifteen in the United States.

The Columbia Records team asked me to do a Q&A with Cohen at Joe's Pub, the club in the Public Theater complex, for New York's press contingent. On a gray and rainy afternoon, *Popular Problems* was played in full for the invited guests, and then I was granted approximately ten minutes for a conversation—obviously not enough to accomplish much of substance, so it seemed best to tee up Leonard, elegant and charming as ever, to do some schtick.

"Getting back on the road has improved my mood considerably," he said, "because I was never good at civilian life."

He brightened when I asked if he intended to follow through on his vow to start smoking again when he turned eighty. "Yes, does anybody have a cigarette?" he said to big laughs. "But quite seriously, does anyone know where you can buy a Turkish or Greek cigarette? I'm looking forward to that first smoke. I've been thinking about that for thirty years. It's one of the few consistent strings of thoughts I've been able to locate."

After the event, I was escorted to his dressing room, where he insisted on pouring me some coffee. We exchanged pleasantries and chatted about Montreal for a few minutes. Cohen seemed in good spirits and, to all appearances, in fine health.

But the truth is that since the conclusion of the *Old Ideas* tour, he had been suffering with physical problems. "Among many other things, he had multiple fractures of the spine," his son, Adam, told *Rolling Stone*. "He has a lot of hard miles on him." In Leonard's own words, his mobility issues left him "confined to barracks" in the Los Angeles house he shared with his daughter, Lorca. But in early 2015, he began working on new music, under very different studio circumstances.

Adam turned Cohen's house into a makeshift recording studio. He put an old Neumann U 87 microphone on the dining room table, filled the living room with computers and gear, and brought in an orthopedic medical chair that would support his father through the many hours of recording. "At times I was very worried about his health, and the only thing that buoyed his spirits was the work itself," said Adam. "And given the incredible and acute discomfort he was suffering from in his largely immobilized state, [creating this album] was a great distraction."

In the interim, having released only two live albums in the first twenty-four years of his career, Cohen added two more to the three he had put out since 2009—the 2014 three-CD set *Live in Dublin* (with a bonus DVD including three additional performances from Canadian shows) and 2015's *Can't Forget: A Souvenir of the Grand Tour*, with ten songs recorded at concerts and sound checks spanning the 2012–2013 dates. Two new compositions were included: one of those, "Got a Little Secret," was taped during the sound check preceding the final show in Auckland.

Leonard and Adam worked on the new album for more than a year. On October 21, 2016, *You Want It Darker* was released. The album was breathtaking—a thirty-six-minute meditation on death and God, shot through with humor, anger, and acceptance. On the opening, searing title track, Cantor Gideon Zelermyer and the choir at Shaar Hashomayim, the Cohen family's Montreal synagogue, deliver an incantation—"Hineni, Hineni / I'm ready, my Lord." The word "Hineni" is a Hebrew word meaning "here I am." It is the response Abraham gives when God calls on him to sacrifice his son Isaac (a tale Cohen explored in 1969's "Story of Isaac" on the *Songs from a Room* album). It is also the name of a prayer of preparation and humility, addressed to God, chanted by the cantor on the high holidays.

In that week's issue of the *New Yorker* magazine, the publication's editor, David Remnick, wrote a lengthy profile of Cohen, drawn from the final interviews that the singer ever gave. "At a certain point, if you still have your marbles and are not faced with serious financial challenges, you have a chance to put your house in order," Cohen said. "Putting your house in order, if you can do it, is one of the most comforting activities, and the benefits of it are incalculable."

Elsewhere, he noted that in his later days, he had "even less and less interest in examining what have got to be very superficial evaluations or opinions about the significance of one's life or one's work," before ultimately offering that in his current state, "I've got some work to do. Take care of business. I am ready to die. I hope it's not too uncomfortable. That's about it for me."

For the piece Remnick also scored a rare interview with Bob Dylan, who offered a surprisingly detailed analysis of Cohen's songwriting structure. Dylan described his Canadian counterpart as "a much more savvy musician than you'd think" and compared him to Irving Berlin ("maybe the only songwriter in modern history that Leonard can be directly related to . . . Berlin was also connected to some kind of celestial sphere").

"When people talk about Leonard, they fail to mention his melodies, which to me, along with his lyrics, are his greatest genius," Dylan said. "Even the counterpoint lines—they give a celestial character and melodic lift to every one of his songs. As far as I know, no one else comes close to this in modern music." (Judy Collins offered a very similar thought in her consideration of "Hallelujah"—"It's so deceptively simple, isn't it? His melodies are often like that. And that's part of the power of how he matches the lyric with the story.")

Remnick asked Dylan about "Hallelujah," the song whose power he had somehow divined before the rest of the world caught up. "That song 'Hallelujah' has resonance for me," Dylan said. "The 'secret chord' and the point-blank I-know-you-better-than-you-know-yourself aspect of the song has plenty of resonance for me."

And then, nineteen days after the release of *You Want It Darker*, Leonard Cohen was gone. He died in his home on November 7, 2016, at the age of eighty-two; leukemia was a contributing cause. According to manager Robert Kory, Cohen's death was the result of a fall at his home on the night of November 7, and he subsequently died in his sleep. Amazingly, Kory and the family were able to keep Cohen's death a secret until November 10, the same day that his funeral was held in Montreal.

You Want It Darker joined a growing library of work in which dying pop stars—George Harrison, Warren Zevon, David Bowie, Gregg Allman—confronted their own mortality and took a shot at a final statement. The titles alone ("Leaving the Table," "Traveling Light") indicated the themes; Cohen's voice, if possible, had grown even deeper, more haunting and more wry, in his final months, and that sound was now left to echo through time.

Tributes to Cohen poured in from around the world. The Canadian prime minister, Justin Trudeau, said he had "managed to reach the highest of artistic achievement. . . . His ability to conjure the vast array of human emotion made him one of the most influential and enduring musicians ever." Benjamin Netanyahu, prime minister of Cohen's beloved Israel, described him as "a great creator" and "a talented artist."

From Lin-Manuel Miranda to Miley Cyrus, J. K. Rowling to Elton John, the outpouring was immense for a man who had spent so many years toiling in relative obscurity to a cult following. Nick Cave wrote that "for many of us Leonard Cohen was the greatest songwriter of them all," and John Cale—whose resculpting of the words to "Hallelujah" set in motion the events that would propel the song into the world—lamented that "the world has one less gentle soul tonight." And on *Billboard*'s December 3 Hot 100 singles chart, there was Leonard's "Hallelujah" for the first time, debuting at Number Fifty-Nine.

Grander tributes came in over time. On the one-year anniversary of his passing, a concert titled "Tower of Song" took place at Montreal's Bell Centre arena. Participants including Sting, Elvis Costello, Lana Del Rey, and Courtney Love performed Cohen songs, while the Shaar Hashomayim choir sang "You Want It Darker" and k.d. lang was tapped to reprise her version of "Hallelujah."

Concurrently, the Musée d'Art Contemporain de Montréal (MAC) organized *Leonard Cohen: A Crack in Everything*, an extensive visual art and multimedia exhibit that was part of the official celebration of the city's 375th anniversary. More than 300,000 visitors attended the exhibit, a record for the museum, and it went on to tour internationally, beginning with a five-month installation at the Jewish Museum in New York. One of the galleries, titled "I Heard There Was a Secret Chord," was a "participatory humming experience" which tracked user data indicating how many people around the world were listening to "Hallelujah" in real time.

There's been a steady flow of books about Cohen since his death, as well, written by friends, colleagues, and critics. They all inevitably grapple with "Hallelujah," and sometimes add to the saga. Judy Scott, who befriended Cohen and

Marianne Ihlen on Hydra, offered this insight into one no-table lyric in 2021's *Leonard, Marianne, and Me*: "Marianne said that Leonard confessed to her that when he was a young child, his mother would insist on cutting his hair. When he got a little older and tried to refuse, she would use one of his father's neckties to tie him to a chair in their kitchen and snip away. Then she'd tell him that, like Sampson [*sic*] in the Bible, Leonard was completely in her power and would have to do anything she asked of him."

The honor that might have amused Cohen the most, though, was probably when the title track of *You Want It Darker* won the Grammy for Best Rock Performance in January 2018 over nominees including Foo Fighters and Chris Cornell. Born with the gift of a golden voice, indeed.

During these years, the Jeff Buckley story didn't change too much. New material—outtakes and live recordings—was steadily released, often to mark anniversaries, whether that meant twenty years since his death in 2017 or, in 2019, twenty-five years since the release of *Grace*. Stories con-stantly continue to celebrate his influence; artists still trum-pet his greatness.

In a recent conversation I had with a nineteen-year-old singer-songwriter named John-Robert (who was signed by Grammy-nominated producer Ricky Reed, who helped develop Lizzo), he suddenly started talking about Buckley. "You can't compare Jeff Buckley to anybody, as a singer or a songwriter," said this artist who was born several years after Buckley's death. "His vocal elasticity, his vibrato is off the charts, he was sinister, beautiful, and haunting at the same time."

Miraculously, though, in 2019, there was a sudden addition to the Leonard Cohen catalogue—an actual new album, *Thanks for the Dance*, made up of vocals that Leonard recorded in his final days, with tracks later completed by Adam Cohen. "In the making of *You Want It Darker*, a theme emerged—mortality, God," Adam told me in a Q&A event I did for Columbia at an audio company's showroom townhouse in SoHo. "It was a goodbye—but that's not the way it started. My father was working on many, many songs simultaneously, and we'd begun many of them. And they weren't discarded because they weren't to his taste; they were discarded because they didn't belong to this theme that was emerging." In his final days, after *You Want It Darker* was released, Leonard gave Adam a mission: "Please, complete the task; finish what we started."

Gathering a group of musical contributors including Jennifer Warnes, producer Daniel Lanois, Leslie Feist, and Bryce Dessner from the National, Adam fleshed out the songs around the riveting recitations Leonard had recorded in his living room. "We saw him delivering these incredible vocals with relative ease, one after another," said Adam, "and I remember saying to him, 'Dad—how are you doing this?' And he said, 'I'm locked in this little apartment—I can't go anywhere, so I have nothing but time to study how each syllable falls.'"

New music was a surprise, but still "Hallelujah" refused to slow down. Every few weeks, to this day, someone sends me a video link to a new performance, another new version from somewhere in the world, and my reply is always the same—"it never stops." Nor do gadflies cease complaining about its over- or misuse. In 2020, *Cracked* (having somehow reinvented itself from low-budget *Mad* magazine imitator to cultural criticism) ran a story titled "The Simple Fix to Prevent Messing Up Your 'Hallelujah' Covers": Unexpectedly, writer Isaac Cabe concentrated on the "large degree of vocal strength" required, and his solution was to emphasize the ¾ ("waltz time") time signature.

Trying to list every new interpretation is futile; only the especially weird ones (a "fan video" Christmas video supporting congresswoman from Hawaii and contrarian presidential candidate Tulsi Gabbard, showing footage of the other Democratic contenders over the line "You don't really care for music, do ya?," or the Montreal Canadiens hockey team opening their 2019 season with a children's choir singing the song) seem worth registering at this point. Though Buckley's version remained the basis for most of these performances (google "Hallelujah" and his video is still the first thing that appears), in 2019, Cohen's own 1984 recording was inducted into the Grammy Hall of Fame.

In February 2020, when the Los Angeles Lakers played their first home game after the death of Kobe Bryant, before the tipoff at the sold-out Staples Center, R&B superstar Usher sang "Amazing Grace." Then the lights came down and a single spotlight illuminated cellist Ben Hong of the LA Philharmonic. He played a solo version of 'Hallelujah" while a video of Bryant speaking about his love of basketball, his family, and the story of his life played on the screens. That same month, k.d. lang performed the song in Sydney for the "Fire Fight Australia" benefit, raising money for relief and recovery from the brushfires that decimated the continent.

And then came the pandemic. "Hallelujah" acted, yet again, as a balm—sung from Italian balconies, in a haunting performance to empty streets in downtown Chicago, by a Cincinnati doctor to his COVID patients during Holy Week. In late 2020, superstar tenor Andrea Bocelli released *Believe*, an album of songs intended to inspire listeners during this most trying time in the world's history, and included "Hallelujah" alongside "Ave Maria," "Amazing Grace," and "You'll Never Walk Alone." He explained the selection to me, saying, "This is a very beautiful song, very nice to listen to, the melody can accompany you the whole day, and it's a song which challenges your faith.

"I think that for every one of us, the relationship with faith is a complex one," Bocelli continued. "The serious one, the authentic faith, it's not an easy journey, it's very hard indeed. Every day, every one of us has this issue that they have to face, and the benefit of this song is exactly this—this aspect is stressed in the song, the complexity of faith."

Nor has the song's stranglehold on televised music competitions abated. In 2020, eleven-year-old cancer survivor Tyler Butler-Figueroa, a violinist, finished in third place on *America's Got Talent*, having advanced to the final round with a solo performance of "Hallelujah" that earned a standing ovation from judges Howie Mandel, Gabrielle Union, Julianne Hough, and—still around after all these years!—Simon Cowell. In August 2021, Arab Israeli singer Valerie Hamaty and Jewish Israeli musician Tamir Grinberg came together onstage for a performance in both Arabic and English on Israel's singing contest *The Next Star* (judges pronounced it the best rendition of all time).

The rise and endurance of "Hallelujah" remains unique, and still something of a mystery. We can break down the component parts of its appeal, but there will never be a logical, much less replicable, explanation. Eric Church compared the song's story to that of the classical composers.

"They weren't popular in the moment, they became popular years later—in some cases, decades later," he said. "And some of that is what happened with 'Hallelujah.' The song didn't really have its one moment. But now, you can go up to anybody and start singing the song, and they're gonna know the song.

"It's almost like the song found its own way. It had nothing to do with him trying to make it a hit, or trying to push it, or trying to do this. It just found its way."

Leonard Cohen didn't speak to me for this book, though he did stun me when he interrupted one of my questions at the 2014 press event for *Popular Problems* and thanked me for writing it. In the limited minutes we had at that event, I asked him something about working on the new album.

"I don't remember much," he said. "When it's finished I develop a benevolent amnesia about the project. We worked diligently for months and, surprisingly, it came to a point of completion. At this point, most things are a blur.

"The thing I cherish about the work," he said, "is the done-ness."

But this is the miracle of "Hallelujah." Almost forty years later, its work is not yet done.

ACKNOWLEDGMENTS

First, an apology: With hundreds of versions of "Hallelujah" floating around out there in audio and video land, it would be foolish to try to cover them all. So if your own favorite performance of the song isn't included in the previous pages, I hope that you at least found some new ways to think about its meaning to you.

Thank you, Leonard Cohen—first, of course, for writing the song, and also for giving this project your blessing. Thanks to Robert Kory for all of the support and assistance. The encouragement and enthusiasm of Tiffany Shipp helped get, and keep, the ball rolling.

Thanks to everyone quoted in these pages for being so generous with their time and thoughts. And thanks to all of the people who helped me speak to such great subjects, and offered insights of their own: Ambrosia Healy, Lori Earl, Lauretta Charlton, Chris Douridas, Perry Greenfield,

Olga Makrias, Ron Shapiro, Sonia Muckle, Josh Page, Char Grant, Jamie Abzug, Sarah Usher, Felice Ecker, Joel Amsterdam, Tom Muzquiz, Dustin Addis, Kevin Chiaramonte, Mark Cunningham, David Brendel, Jack Rovner, Cem Kurosman, Fran DeFeo, Meredith Plant, Mary Moyer, Sarah Avrin, David Browne, Suzanne Lang Middaugh, Ramon Parkins, and Seth Faber.

Love and deepest gratitude to Jennifer Goldsmith Adams and Emily Zemler for introductions, input, and everything else.

I still can't quite believe that Peter Borland at Atria read the proposal for this strange little book, immediately understood it, and said, "Just go do it." His confidence in me and in my premise was remarkable. Also at Atria, thanks to Daniel Loedel, David Brown, Valerie Vennix, Sean deLone, Steve Breslin, and Liz Byer.

My gratitude, respect, and love to Dayna Goldfine and Dan Geller and everyone at Geller/Goldfine Productions. You found new layers to this story for *Hallelujah: Leonard Cohen, a Journey, a Song*—it's been inspiring to watch the film develop and a pleasure to work on it with you, and I'm so proud to be a part of it.

Sarah Lazin is so much more than an agent—she is a friend, an editor, and a fount of wisdom, and I'm so lucky that she puts up with me. Thanks also to Manuela Jessel, and to Laura Nolan and Catharine Strong at Aevitas Creative.

From before Day One, Alice White Bezanson was a necessary cheerleader ("Rock Chalk," etc.) for this idea. She then went on to be a transcriber, researcher, and fact-checker extraordinaire, and a valuable second set of eyes whenever I needed one.

Everyone at Artists Den Entertainment—Mark Lieberman, Anji Chandra, Devon Wambold, Clare Flynn, and John Hanle—allowed me the space and time to get this thing done, while they also kept busy producing the best live music on television. And thanks to Mark Goodman, Kerry Alivizatos, Jake Vevera, Roger Coletti, and everyone at SiriusXM Volume for making daily radio an unlikely new way to tell stories about music.

For all that they've taught me about writing and music and writing about music, eternal gratitude to Anthony De-Curtis, Sia Michel, Diane Cardwell, and Danyel Smith.

For too many reasons to mention, love and thanks to Hal Brooks, Keith Hammond, Mike Paranzino, Dick Schumacher, Mike Errico, Dan Carey, James Shifren, Bronwen Hruska, Johanna Schlegel, Shannon Carey, Sam Kramer, Rob Johnson, Sarah Wilson, Elysa Gardner, and Joe Angio.

Love always to Irwin, Janet, and Sharon Light, my perfect family who always encouraged me to make a life and a career out of the things I most cared about as a teenager.

This book, like everything I do every day, is for Suzanne McElfresh and Adam Light. You are the reason for my hallelujah.

Selected "Hallelujah" Discography

Hundreds of artists have performed the song live (Bob Dylan, Regina Spektor, U2, etc.), and many hundreds more have posted videos on YouTube. There are also numerous other recordings, but this list includes only those versions that were commercially released and were mentioned within the preceding pages.

Leonard Cohen, *Various Positions,* 1984, Columbia

John Cale, *I'm Your Fan: The Songs of Leonard Cohen,* 1991, EastWest

John Cale, *Fragments of a Rainy Season* (live album), 1992, Hannibal

Jeff Buckley, *Grace,* 1994, Columbia

Leonard Cohen, *Cohen Live,* 1994, Columbia

Bono, *Tower of Song: The Songs of Leonard Cohen,* 1995, A&M

Rufus Wainwright, *Shrek: Music from the Original Motion Picture* (soundtrack), 2001, DreamWorks

Chris Botti, *December,* 2002, Sony

Jeff Buckley, *Live at Sin-é (Legacy Edition),* 2003, Columbia

Allison Crowe, *Tidings,* 2004, Rubenesque

k. d. lang, *Hymns of the 49th Parallel,* 2004, Nonesuch

Rufus Wainwright, *Live at the Fillmore* (bonus DVD included with his album *Want Two*), 2004, DreamWorks

Popa Chubby, *Big Man Big Guitar: Popa Chubby Live,* 2005, Blind Pig

Espen Lind, Askil Holm, Kurt Nilsen, and Alejandro Fuentes, *Hallelujah—Live,* 2006, Playroom

Willie Nelson, *Songbird,* 2006, Lost Highway

Fall Out Boy, *Infinity on High* (sampled on "Hum Hallelujah"), 2007, Island

Alexandra Burke, "Hallelujah" (*X Factor* performance), 2008, Sony

Il Divo, *The Promise,* 2008, Syco

Kate Voegele, "Hallelujah" (digital single), 2008, MySpace/ Interscope

Michael McDonald, *Soul Speak,* 2008, Universal

Paramore, *The Final Riot!* (live CD/DVD; introduction to their own song, also called "Hallelujah"), 2008, Fueled by Ramen

Alexandra Burke, *Overcome,* 2009, Sony

The Canadian Tenors, *The Canadian Tenors,* 2009, Universal

Leonard Cohen, *Live in London* (CD/DVD), 2009, Columbia

Bon Jovi, *Live at Madison Square Garden* (DVD), 2010, Island

Jason Castro, *Jason Castro,* 2010, Atlantic

Justin Timberlake (with Matt Morris and Charlie Sexton), *Hope for Haiti Now* (digital album), 2010, MTV

k. d. lang, *Hallelujah* (EP; includes iTunes Exclusive Vancouver Winter Olympics version), 2010, Nonesuch

Lee DeWyze, "Hallelujah" (*American Idol* performance; iTunes single), 2010, 19 Recordings

Leonard Cohen, *Songs from the Road* (DVD), 2010, Columbia

Neil Diamond, *Dreams,* 2010, Columbia

Renée Fleming, *Dark Hope,* 2010, Decca

Susan Boyle, *The Gift*, 2010, Syco

Brandi Carlile, *Live at Benaroya Hall with the Seattle Symphony*, 2011, Columbia

Jake Shimabukuro, *Peace Love Ukulele*, 2011, Hitchhike

Michael Bolton, *Gems: The Duets Collection*, 2011, Legacy

Damien Rice, *Rock and Roll Hall of Fame Volume 10: 2008-2009*, 2011, Direct Holdings

Judy Collins and Bhi Bhiman, *Strangers Again*, 2015, Wildflower

Tori Kelly, *Sing: Original Motion Picture Soundtrack*, 2016, Republic

Eric Church, *Mr. Misunderstood on the Rocks: Live and (Mostly) Unplugged*, 2017, EMI Nashville

Pentatonix, *A Pentatonix Christmas*, 2017, RCA

Lindsey Stirling, *Warmer in the Winter*, 2018, Lindseystomp/Concord

Andrea Bocelli, *Believe*, 2020, Decca

INDEX

CPSIA information can be obtained
at www.ICGtesting.com
Printed in the USA
BVHW031555050522
635518BV00003B/3